STU

A Cri

STUMPED?

A Cricket Quiz

Christopher Martin-Jenkins

ORBIS ● LONDON

First published
in Great Britain
by Orbis Publishing
Limited, London 1984

© Christopher Martin-Jenkins 1984

ISBN: 0-85613-673-5

All rights reserved. No part of this
publication may be reproduced, stored
in a retrieval system or transmitted in
any form or by any means electronic,
mechanical photocopying, recording or
otherwise, without the prior permission
of the publishers. Such permission, if
granted, is subject to a fee depending on
the nature of the use.
Printed in Great Britain.

Devised by Orbis Publishing Limited
Designed and produced by Michael Balfour Limited
Designer: Hilly Beavan
Cover illustration: Roy Ullyett
Typesetting: Project Reprographics
Printed in Great Britain

CONTENTS

	Preface	7
1.	History	9
2.	Personalities	21
3.	Elimination	43
4.	Horror Stretches	47
5.	Achievements	53
6.	All-Rounders in Other Fields	77
7.	Domestic Competitions	85
8.	Art and Literature	95
9.	Broadcasting and Journalists	103
10.	Records	107
11.	The Laws	115
12.	Extras	121
	The Answers	129

PREFACE

Cricket is a game whose action extends far beyond the confines of the playing area, and whose events stay alive for several thousands of times the duration of even a five-day Test match. Cricket is rich in personalities, records, events and history; it has formed its own literature and its own forms of journalism. It has produced players who have easily acquired statesmanship on their retirement, and even its Laws — so baffling to the outsider — are a constant source of passionate debate and intense speculation.

This book is offered as an arena for testing and enhancing your knowledge of the facts, characters and arcana of cricket. I hope it will prolong your pleasure of the game into the long hours after stumps are drawn, and provide an amusing way of pitching your knowledge against that of your fellow cricket-lovers. Each of these thirteen quizzes has been designed in a sequence, with gentler deliveries at the beginning leading on to more challenging and demanding ones — with some real snorters to probe even the securest defences. Anyone who can answer more than ninety per cent of the Laws quiz should consider applying to be put on the umpires' roll! Anyone who can get more than ninety per cent of the personalities quiz right could look forward to a career as a commentator. . . while anyone who can answer over ninety per cent of *Stumped?* correctly has obviously never had time to play the game!

I am much indebted to the kind assistance of Chris Rhys, James Coldham and David Whiley for supplying various questions and answers and checking others. All three have contributed chanceless innings; if anyone is now found to have been caught in the slips it is me.

Christopher Martin-Jenkins

FIRST QUIZ
HISTORY

1. Which ground staged the first Test match in 1877?

2. Where, currently, are the 'Ashes'?

3. Which of the Ionian Islands still plays cricket following its introduction there by Britons in the mid-19th century?

4. What match was played for the last time at Lord's in 1962?

5. Why is the Sheffield Shield so called?

6. How many balls were there in an over when the first Laws of Cricket were drawn up?

7. Originally there were only two stumps: was the batsman out if the ball passed between the stumps?

8. What do the I Zingari, Free Foresters and XL Clubs all have in common?

9. Which is the most active cricketing country on the European mainland?

10. Who captained the first Australian team to tour England?

11. Which country withdrew from the 1979 Prudential World Cup preliminary round because 'they could not raise a good enough team'?

12. In which country is the 'Castle Bowl' competition

i   The 1878 Australian touring team to England. How many of them can you identify?

FIRST QUIZ: HISTORY

contested by cricketers?

13. Which two countries contest the 'Frank Worrell' Trophy?

14. For which two teams did Sir Donald Bradman play in the Sheffield Shield?

15. In 1867 where did MCC play a match outside the United Kingdom?

16. Which two countries were involved in the first 'International' match in 1844?

17. What two cities have staged Test matches at three different centres?

18. Which ground became the 50th Test centre in 1979?

19. Which was the first country to lose nineteen wickets to catches in one Test match?

20. Which nine counties took part in the first 'official' county championship in 1873?

21. Richard Nyren and the village of Hambledon both played their part in the early development of cricket in England. What was the name of the Inn in Hambledon of which Nyren was landlord?

22. Sri Lanka was accepted as a full member of the Test and County Cricket Board in 1981. What two other countries were elected as associate members at the same meeting?

23. Who were (a) The Doctor (e) The Black Bradman
    (b) The Coroner (f) 'Shrimp'
    (c) The Demon (g) The Terror
    (d) The Big Ship (h) 'Iron Gloves'?

24. The inaugural Lambert & Butler floodlight competition was held in 1981. On which ground did Lancashire beat Leicestershire in the final?

25. Due to fixture congestion, the 1979 Varsity Match was moved from Lord's for the first time in 150 years — where was it played?

26. Which two countries contest the W.J. Jordan trophy?

27. The 'Grace Gates' can be found at Lord's, and at which other county ground?

28. Apart from Glamorgan, which three Welsh counties have competed in either the County Championship or the Minor Counties Championship?

29. When and where did a team from the West Indies first go on tour?

30. Who was the first man to hit the ball over the present Lord's pavilion?

31. (a) Which major touring team to England was captained by a Maharajah, and what was his name?
    (b) Who was sent home from the tour for indiscipline?

32. Which side in 1979 became the first winners of the I.C.C. Trophy?

33. Which fast bowler was known as 'Foghorn' and for which team, mainly, did he play?

34. Who was the last leg-spin bowler to top the Australian first-class bowling averages, and when?

35. What was the name of the first women's cricket club, formed in 1887?

36. What was the name of the downs on which the famous Hambledon Club played during the 18th century?

37. Where was the floodlit cricket match held in 1947 for Denis Compton's benefit?

38. Who contested the first known county match, when and where?

39. On which current county ground was there evidence of a greyhound track until 1979?

40. The first cricket laws were drawn up in 1744 as a result of a meeting of which club?

41. Of which club was the White Conduit Club a forerunner?

42. Which batsman is credited with the first ever recorded century?

43. Lord's was forced to move to its present site in 1815. Why?

44. (a) When were eight-ball overs introduced into Australian domestic cricket?
    (b) When were six-ball overs last re-introduced?

45. At which current county ground was a forty-five pound salmon once caught?

46. Which was the only animal to have its obituary printed in *Wisden's Cricketer's Almanack*?

47. Who scored 181 in Australia's first innings in the tied Test between Australia and the West Indies in 1960?

48. The first recorded cricket match in Ireland took place in Dublin in 1792. Where was the match played?

FIRST QUIZ: HISTORY

49. Which two events of importance to cricket occurred in 1744?

50. Who opened the batting for Australia in their first Test in England in 1880?

ii Two men look forward to the start of an historic tour.
 (a) What is the tour?
 (b) Who are they both?

iii Colin Cowdrey and a fellow English batsman make their way at the double to the pavilion at the end of a Lord's

FIRST QUIZ: HISTORY 17

Test. Why is Cowdrey's arm in plaster. Who is the other batsman and why is there so much excitement?

iv   A West Indian eleven being led out at Lords in 1944 by a famous Lancashire baron.

FIRST QUIZ: HISTORY

(a) Who is he?
(b) Who is the Test player on his left?

v   Who are these former England players? Why are they outside the Home Office, and in what capacities?

SECOND QUIZ
PERSONALITIES

1. Which famous test cricketer had the second Christian name of 'St Aubrun'?

2. Who was the youngest person to appear in a Test match, at the age of fifteen years 124 days in 1958?

3. Which English cricketer added a third forename, 'Dylan', by deed poll because of his admiration for singer/songwriter Bob Dylan?

4. Which five non-wicketkeepers have taken over 800 catches in first-class cricket?

5. By what name was Mansur Ali Khan better known?

6. Who is the 1983 England Test cricketer whose house is named 'Hambledon' after the famous early cricketing village?

7. Which first class cricketer, playing in 1984, has the same surname as that of a first-class county?

8. Whom did Geoff Boycott succeed as captain of Yorkshire?

9. Which Australian cricketer was christened 'Durtanovitch' but subsequently changed his name?

10. Which Lancashire player was the first 'Young Cricketer of the Year' in 1950?

11. Which man made his debut for England in the 1980 Centenary Test?

12. Playing Test cricket for his county is the highlight of every player's career. Which player rated it so highly that he cancelled his wedding in 1984 in order to play for England on tour?

13. Which man, twenty-three years after making his first-class debut, scored his maiden first class double century, in 1980?

14. Which man was involved in the 'aluminium bat' affair with the umpires during the 1979-1980 Australia-England series?

15. Which batsman once scored 2,000 runs in a season for fourteen consecutive seasons?

16. Who captained Australia in their first Test match?

17. Which famous cricketer had the nickname of 'The Croucher'?

18. Which man took over the Australian captaincy immediately after Richie Benaud?

19. The great Sydney Barnes played for three different counties including Warwickshire and Lancashire. What is the third?

20. Who was Australia's captain when Jim Laker ran riot at Old Trafford in 1956?

21. In putting on 128 for England's last wicket in the fifth Test against West Indies in 1966, which two men scored their maiden first-class fifties in the process?

22. Name the two former England Test captains who played in their final Test match against the West Indies at Old Trafford in 1976?

SECOND QUIZ: PERSONALITIES

23. Which bowler holds the distinction of taking the most first-class wickets in *one* decade — 2,058?

24. Which present-day Test cricketer is known as the 'Haryana Hurricane'?

25. Which man took three wickets in four balls on *two occasions* during the 1972 England-Australia series?

26. Who scored his one and only Test century for England against the West Indies at Nottingham in 1976?

27. Who was the 'Brylcreem boy' and why?

28. (a) Who captained Yorkshire for 28 seasons and in which years?
    (b) What made him unusual amongst Yorkshire players?

29. Who was the only Australian cricketer to play for the Rest of the World in the 1970 series against England?

30. (a) Who was flown out as a replacement for the injured Bob Willis on the 1980-81 tour of the West Indies?
    (b) Whom did Willis replace on the 1970-71 tour of Australia?

31. Which England cricketer became a father while on the 1978-79 tour of Australia?

32. Who captained Australia in the 'Bodyline' series?

33. Who was England's wicketkeeper immediately after Godfrey Evans?

34. Apart from being Test cricketers, what do the following have in common: Richard Hadlee, Brian Close, Brian Statham, Jack Flavell, Graham Dilley and Clive Lloyd?

i   Name this man who first played for his county as a bowler, batting number 11, but whose diligent net practice seems to have paid off!

ii Who is this man, one of the most glorious left-handers of post-war years, and who is the Middlesex fielder?

35. Who succeeded Rachael Heyhoe-Flint as captain of the England Ladies team in 1977?

36. Who opened England's batting with Mike Brearley in the Centenary Test against Australia at Melbourne in 1977?

37. Who is the only player to have achieved the double of 1,000 runs and 100 wickets in his *first* season in first-class cricket?

38. For which team did Gary Sobers play when he brought his skills to the Central Lancashire League in 1975?

39. Who made his Test debut for England in 1946, despite having only eleven first-class matches to his credit?

40. Which recent England Test cricketer was nicknamed 'The Shoreditch Sparrow' and who was the writer who so dubbed him?

41. In which country was the England batsman Bob Woolmer born?

42. Who, with 10,232 runs, has scored the most first-class runs of Australian players not selected for their country?

43. Who amongst left-handers has scored most runs for Australia?

44. What were the names of the four Mohammed brothers who played for Pakistan?

45. What was Dennis Lillee's nickname?

46. Which England captain won a half-blue for Lacrosse?

47. (a) Who announced his retirement from Test cricket in an interview with his brother?

(b) When had he previously announced his retirement from Test cricket?

48. Which post-war England captain was born in Peru, and during the Second World War was captured at Tobruk and subsequently returned to England some four and a half stones lighter?

49. Who played the last of his twenty-two Tests for England in the first Test match to be staged at Trent Bridge?

50. Which man has captained England to the greatest number of wins in Test cricket?

51. Which 1983 first-class cricketer was born in Maracaibo, Venezuela?

52. Which batsman caused a stir at Old Trafford in 1979 when he threw his bat through a dressing-room window in disgust?

53. What are the surname and initials of the three brothers who all played in the 1891-92 South Africa-England Test match at Cape Town — *two* for England and *one* for South Africa?

54. Who scored England's first post-war Test century?

55. Who scored 249 not out for Holkar in the 1944-45 Ranji Trophy in India?

56. Which post-war England captain once stated he was unavailable for an MCC tour of South Africa because of his political involvement?

57. Which batsman has scored the most runs in any post-war decade?

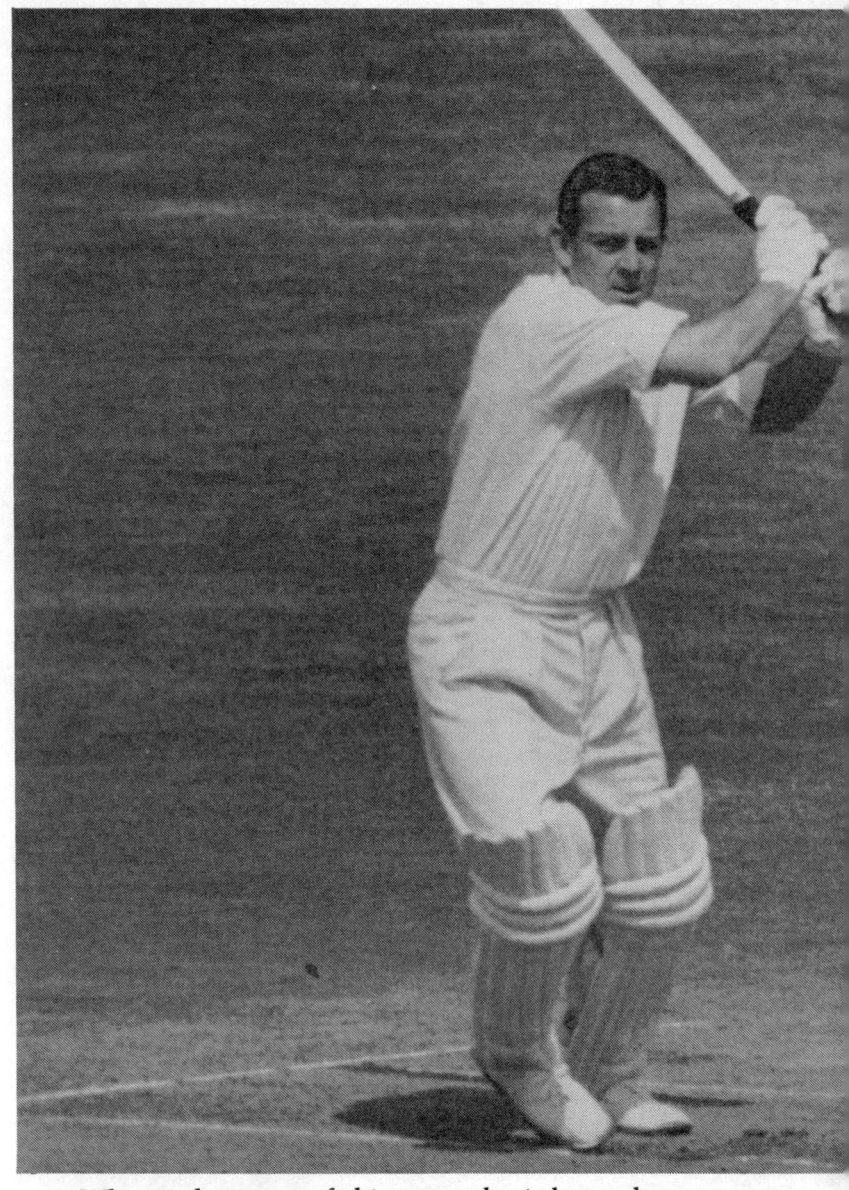

iii What is the name of this man who is better known on the other side of the stumps?

SECOND QUIZ: PERSONALITIES

58. Which batsman holds the all-time record for scoring the most runs in *any* one decade?

59. Which man holds the record for taking the most wickets in any post-war decade?

60. Who was the New Zealand batsman on the receiving end of the Trevor Chappell 'underarm' ball during the controversial one-day Test in 1981?

61. (a) Which umpire once withdrew himself for one over during an England-West Indies Test match at Edgbaston?
    (b) Why?

62. Which Australian batsman, and occasionally controversial bowler of the fifties, shot himself in 1979?

63. Which wicketkeeper made his Test debut for England the same day that Colin Cowdrey was making *his* Test debut?

64. Who is the only Lancastrian player to have scored a Test century for England at Old Trafford?

65. (a) Which Lancashire player scored a century in an Old Trafford Test for another country?
    (b) When?

66. When 'Old England' met 'Old Australia' in the match at The Oval which preceded the Centenary Test in 1980, who in fact was the oldest of all the players taking part?

67. (a) Who was the first Indian to score a century in each innings of a Test match?
    (b) When and against whom?

68. Which former West Indies Test player was manager of

the team which won the 1979 Prudential World Cup?

69. Who was Gary Sobers' first Test victim, and the man who was to write his biography?

70. Which Australian Test bowler was known as 'Tangles'?

71. What is the name of Clive Lloyd's cousin who has represented the West Indies on many occasions?

72. Which famous England player made his final Test appearance on 2nd July 1935, when South Africa defeated England for the first time, winning by 157 runs at Lords?

73. Which England bowler made his debut in the match that was Fred Trueman's last, against New Zealand at Lords in 1965?

74. Name the two *future* England captains who made their debuts in the fourth Test against New Zealand at Old Trafford in 1958.

75. Which man played in every one of Pakistan's Test matches from their first game in 1952, up to the third Test at Headingley in 1962?

76. Who was the last man to captain England on his *Test debut?*

77. Which man, during the same match in 1980, reached two personal milestones: 20,000 first-class runs, and 1,000 first-class wickets?

78. A famous umpire's Christian names were Albert Ennion Growcott, but what was the simpler name by which he was known?

iv A fast left-hander, this coach once dismissed O'Brien, Bradman and McCabe in four balls. Who is he?

SECOND QUIZ: PERSONALITIES 33

v   Name the bowler, the wicketkeeper, the slip and the unfortunate batsman in this photograph of an unusual combination of players. What is especially significant about the latter?

79. (a) Which family had a father who played in one Test for England in 1937, and a son who played in 46 Tests between 1954 and 1968?
    (b) What unique feat did the father achieve?
    (c) In which year?

80. Who took all ten wickets, all bowled, in a first-class match, where and when?

81. In each of two separate Test matches against England three New Zealand batsmen have scored individual hundreds in the same innings. Who were the six batsmen, on what grounds and in which years?

82. Which professional cricketer had a memorial service in Westminster Abbey?

83. (a) Which 1983 first-class cricketer is the son of Lord and Lady Rochester?
    (b) For what three first-class teams did he play?

84. Who once took 100 wickets or more in a season on twenty consecutive occasions in first-class cricket, and also holds the distinction of being the only Dorset player to have won a Gillette Cup Man of the Match award?

85. Who were the two members of the 1969 New Zealand Test team who refused to play cricket on a Sunday because of their religious beliefs?

86. Which County cricketer became a father for the first time during a 1984 match at Northampton and a few hours after the birth found himself in the same hospital next door to his wife with a broken thumb?

87. (a) For what is the Walter Lawrence Trophy awarded?

(b) Who was the first man to win the Trophy twice and in which years?

88. (a) Who was the first man ever to be prevented from bowling for delivering too many short balls? This occurred in the third Pakistan-New Zealand Test in 1976-77.
(b) Who was the batsman in this instance?
(c) Who was the umpire?
(d) Who was the captain of the fielding side?

89. Who was the Australian batsman felled by John Snow in the 1970-71 Test at Sydney, provoking an incident which eventually led Ray Illingworth to lead the England team off the field?

90. Which England cricketer scored his one and only Test century against New Zealand in 1950-51?

91. Which Somerset player scored the first century in the John Player League?

92. Which South African had the Christian names Norman Bertram Fleetwood, and what was his nickname?

93. For which Lancashire League team did Dennis Lillee play in 1971?

94. Which former Lancashire player scored his one and only Test century against Australia in 1965-66?

95. Who is the youngest man ever to have captained England in a Test match?

96. Who is the only woman to have appeared in the list of births and deaths in *Wisden*?

97. Who is the *oldest* man to have hit a post-war century for England in a Test match?

vi England v New Zealand at Lords in 1965. Name the players in the photograph.

SECOND QUIZ: PERSONALITIES

98. Who was the last Essex player before Keith Fletcher to have captained England?

99. Who played for the Minor Counties in the 1980 Benson & Hedges Cup, and later in the season for the West Indies *against* the Minor Counties?

100. Who scored two Test centuries for England: one against the West Indies at Lords in 1969, and the other against India at Old Trafford in 1971?

101. Who holds the record for scoring most runs in the Sheffield Shield?

102. What is the name of the only Cornishman to have played Test cricket for England?

103. Two pairs of brothers have scored post-war Test centuries for Australia. Greg and Ian Chappell were one; who were the other pair?

104. What do the former Surrey players Stuart Surridge and John Shuter have in common?

105. Who made his Middlesex debut in 1981, one day after his thirty-eighth birthday?

106. Who had his jaw broken by a bouncer from Bob Willis in the Centenary Test at Melbourne in 1977?

107. What is the name of the late England captain whose daughter is married to Peter May?

108. What significant part did Richie Benaud, J. Courie and J.B. Stollmeyer play in Len Hutton's career?

109. Which Australian cricketer was known as 'The Governor-General'?

SECOND QUIZ: PERSONALITIES

110. Who took fifty-five Sheffield Shield wickets for South Australia in 1982-83?

111. Who was the spin bowler who made his Test debut for the West Indies in the second Test with Pakistan in 1980-81 — their first spin bowler in nine Tests?

112. Indian Test cricketer Kapil Dev replaced which Australian Test player at Haslingden in the Lancashire League?

113. Who was the West Indian fast bowler in the 1930's who was executed in 1955 for the murder of his wife?

114. What were the names of the two English players, in the Kingston Test of the 1929-30 series with the West Indies, who were both over the age of fifty?

115. Who was the first cricketer to receive in excess of £100,000 from a benefit?

116. Which future Australian Test captain played for Accrington in 1959?

117. Who, in 1980, became the first umpire for 24 years to stand in a Test match without having previously played first-class cricket?

118. Which famous Australian fast bowler later made a successful career as a florist?

119. Who performed a hat trick for England but failed to score in his only two first-class innings for Essex?

120. Which Australian Test player had the second name of Byron?

vii In this man's early days he was a batsman/wicketkeeper, and many of his later victims would have wished that he had remained that way. Who is he?

viii (a) Who is this master of leg spin?
(b) Who is the umpire?

ix The Australian team at Lords in 1968. Name all the players and identify the captain?

121. Who was Neil Adcock's partner in South Africa's most feared fast bowling combination?

122. Which Warwickshire and Glamorgan cricketer became known as 'Dai Peroxide'?

123. What was the nickname of the captain of the 1919 Australian Imperial Forces team in England?

124. Who began life at Downend and ended it at Elmers End?

125. Whose bowling action was described by Ian Peebles as resembling that of a 'policeman using his truncheon to strike the head of a particularly short offender'?

THIRD QUIZ
ELIMINATION

From the nine answers given, eliminate eight from the clues. Which one are you left with?

Players 1

1. Has over seventy consecutive Test matches to his name.
2. He reached the milestone of 35,000 first class runs in 1982.
3. Captain of Glamorgan the day Gary Sobers hit six sixes off Malcolm Nash.
4. Played in fifty-two Test matches.
5. Toured Australia twice.
6. Reached the milestone of 35,000 runs in 1983.
7. Awarded his county cap in 1963.
8. Played for Warwickshire and Lancashire as well as his country.

(a) Clive Lloyd
(b) Sunil Gavaskar
(c) W.G. Grace
(d) Tony Lewis
(e) Bob Barber
(f) Dennis Amiss
(g) Don Bradman
(h) Geoff Boycott
(i) Alan Jones

Players 2

1. Played for Yorkshire and Derbyshire.

(a) Brian Statham

2. Has over 5,000 Test runs and over 200 Test wickets to his name. (b) Titch Freeman

3. An overseas-born captain of England. (c) Viv Richards

4. Once bowled 774 balls in a Test match. (d) Kapil Dev

5. At one time played for Pudsey St Lawrence. (e) Tony Greig

6. Has 252 wickets in seventy Test matches. (f) Tony Lock

7. Holds the record for most wickets in a career in the County Championship. (g) John Snow

8. Played in the qualifying tournament of soccer's World Cup. (h) Sonny Ramadhin

   (i) Fred Trueman

Countries

1. The Eden Gardens Ground can be found here. (a) India

2. Ted Dexter's country of birth. (b) Albania

3. Dismissed for the lowest score in the Prudential World Cup. (c) New Zealand

4. Kapil Dev scored 175 against them in 1983 World Cup. (d) West Indies

5. England contest the Wisden Trophy with them. (e) Denmark

6. Finished third in the Women's World Cup in both 1978 and 1982 (f) Canada

7. C.B. Fry once declined to be king here. (g) Zimbabwe

8. A Derbyshire opening bowler comes from here. (h) Italy

(i) Kenya

Grounds

1. Where Alec Bedser once took fourteen for ninety-nine in a Test match. (a) Lord's

2. Has connections with a Yorkshire landowner. (b) Trent Bridge

3. Scene of only one Test match. (c) Cape Town

4. Where Cedric Rhodes is at home. (d) Old Trafford

5. Home of the WACA. (e) Durban

6. First used as a Test centre in 1888-89, and still used today. (f) Bramall Lane

7. Home of the Ellis Park ground. (g) Adelaide

8. Where Eddie Barlow scored 201 in 1963-64. (h) Johannesburg

(i) Perth

FOURTH QUIZ

HORROR STRETCHES

1. During the 1952 series with England, who lost their first four wickets for no runs in the first Test at Headingley and in the fourth Test at the Oval found themselves with five wickets down for the much improved total of six?

2. In the 1978-79 Australia-England series the opening Australian partnership in the first innings of each of the six Tests was broken by a run-out. Which batsman figured in all six?

3. Who were bowled out for fifteen by whom at Melbourne in 1903-04?

4. Who was out first ball when the Australians scored their record 721 in a day against Essex in 1948?

5. Which player, who later became a Test centurion, was dismissed for a 'pair' in his first Test for England in 1975?

6. Which country finished bottom of the County Championship with the exception of only three years between 1930 and 1948?

7. Which country has been bowled out on four of the six occasions when a country has been dismissed for forty or less in a Test match?

8. Which side, in a County championship match, was once dismissed for fifteen runs in the first innings, scored 521 following on in the second and duly won the match by 155 runs?

9. Who played in eight first-class matches on a tour of England and was bowled for nought by the only ball he faced?

10. Who beat the 1977 Australian touring team at Ashbrooke in Sunderland?

11. When England scored their record 903 for seven declared against Australia in 1938, which one of their batsmen was dismissed for a duck?

12. When five Australians scored centuries in the 755 for eight total against the West Indies at Kingston in 1954-55, who was the unfortunate batsman who scored nought?

13. (a) Which team was once dismissed by Natal for totals of sixteen and eighteen in a Currie Cup match?
    (b) When?

14. (a) Who was dismissed for a 'five and nought' when he was making his 'England' debut against the Rest of the World?
    (b) How many more times did he play for England?

15. In a Test match in 1975-76, which country batted through their second innings with five men absent through injury?

16. Which team was dismissed by Gloucestershire for only twelve runs in the 1907 County Championship, and for fifteen runs by Yorkshire the following year?

17. (a) Which Australian bowler once took one wicket for 298 runs in a Test innings?
    (b) In which match?

18. In the first Test between India and Australia in 1977-78, which batsman was dismissed when his cap fell off and dislodged the bails?

19. Gary Sobers once hit Malcolm Nash for thirty-six runs

off one over, but who hit him for thirty-four in a County Championship match in 1977?

20. When England beat Australia in the seventh Test at Sydney in 1971 Ian Chappell had taken over from Bill Lawry as captain, but who replaced Lawry to win his only cap as opening bat?

21. The fifth Test between the West Indies and Australia at Kingston in 1977-78 ended in chaos — and a draw. As there was a riot on the final day's play which left thirty-eight balls unplayed it was decided to play them the next day, but the authorities omitted to tell the umpires officially. Which umpire consequently did not arrive for the final session until it was too late?

22. Victoria scored their record 1,107 runs in an innings in the 1926-27 season, yet when they played the same opponents four weeks later they were dismissed for under 100. What was their total and who were their opponents?

23. Which man in the 1978 Prudential Trophy match at Old Trafford between England and New Zealand had the double distinction of scoring the fastest ever fifty in the competition and having the most uneconomical bowling figures in the competition, when he returned figures of none for eighty-four?

24. When South Africa beat Australia in all four Tests in 1970, which bowler had the following record: none for seventy-four and none for twenty-nine in the first Test, none for ninety-two in the second Test, did not play in the third Test and none for sixty-six and one for seventy-two in the fourth Test?

25. Which countries, and between what years, have suffered:
    (a) the most consecutive defeats? (Two countries).
    (b) the most consecutive matches without victory?

26. Which bowler, in a 1982 County Championship game, bowled an eighteen-ball over, which included eleven no balls and one wide?

27. Who batted through a full day of Test cricket for the least number of runs? When and against whom?

28. During 'Laker's Test' at Old Trafford in 1956, who was the only Australian batsman dismissed for a 'pair'?

29. What is the lowest first-class innings total? (Three possible answers.)

30. When Len Hutton was dismissed for 'obstructing the field' against the South Africans in 1951, how exactly was he obstructing the field?

31. Who scored ninety-nine on his debut for Australia against England in 1934 and went on to play fourteen Tests, but never scored a Test century?

32. What was unique about Peter Judge's two innings in Glamorgan's match against the Indians in 1946?

33. Which bowler was hit for six consecutive sixes by Mike Procter in a county championship game in 1979?

34. Up to 1983 which county had appeared in four one-day finals at Lords and lost them all?

35. Which player reached 250 in a Test match, and could have added even further to his total had he not been out 'hit wicket'?

36. Who was the last bowler to dismiss Geoff Boycott for a duck in a Test match?

37. Which bowler conceded over 300 runs in a Test match

on two occasions?

38. Australian batsman Rick Darling was given life-saving treatment during the 1978-79 fifth Test with England, following a delivery from whom?

39. Who was the first batsman to have been left on ninety-nine not out in a Test match?

40. Fred Titmus was the last man to perform the double of 1,000 runs and 100 wickets in an English season, but who has come nearest since then, with 107 wickets and 959 runs?

41. Which bowler dismissed Don Bradman for a duck in his last Test innings, thus depriving him of a final Test average of 100?

42. Which bowler in spite of performing the hat trick in the 1974 Benson & Hedges Cup final ended up on the losing side?

43. Who scored 7,624 Test runs although he never scored a double century?

44. Which batsman scored 107 and fifty-six on his Test debut in 1972-73 but never played in another Test match?

45. Which minor county failed by only two runs in 1978 to become the first minor county to reach the third round of the Gillette Cup when they were beaten by Sussex, the eventual winners of the trophy?

46. Which West Indian bowler did Haslingden sack at the end of the 1978 season?

47. Which first-class county holds the 'record' for going six

seasons without winning a Gillette Cup match, and when?

48. Which team on the final day of a John Player League season when they needed three runs off the final ball to tie their match and thus win the title, only scored two and failed?

49. What first-class cricketer received his county cap in 1979 and was sacked two weeks later?

50. What was the immediate effect of the events of 1789 on cricket?

i   Who are the umpires, and why are they likely to recall this as one of the worst days of their life?

FIFTH QUIZ
ACHIEVEMENTS

Batting

1. Who in the first Test with the West Indies in 1980-81, was the Pakistani who scored his maiden Test century on his twenty-eighth birthday, and at the same time became only the second Pakistani to score 1,000 Test runs and take 100 Test wickets?

2. Who hit a record number of eighteen centuries in the 1947 season?

3. (a) Which is the only Test ground to have had three Test triple centuries scored on it?
   (b) By whom?

4. Which three Australian batsmen have scored triple centuries in Tests against England — the inevitable Bradman, Bob Cowper and who else?

5. Which Australian-born Test umpire scored over 3,000 runs in the 1961 English season?

6. Which batsman scored over 2,000 runs every season from 1922 to 1935?

7. Which Somerset batsman hit seventy-two sixes in 1935?

8. Who won the man of the match award in the 1980 Centenary Test at Lords, following innings of 117 and eighty-four?

9. Who is the only man to have carried his bat throughout a complete Test innings for New Zealand? When and against whom did he twice perform this feat?

i   This is one of a famous Australian cricketing family.
    (a) Who is he?
    (b) What Test record did he hold for several years?
    (c) Which of his relatives also played for Australia?

FIFTH QUIZ: ACHIEVEMENTS

ii An all-rounder, this man developed a delivery that in Australia bears his name.
   (a) Who is he?
   (b) What are the Australian and English terms for his invention?
   (c) For what was his son, who died in 1984, famous?

iii Why might Tony Lock have had complex feelings about taking this catch?

FIFTH QUIZ: ACHIEVEMENTS

10. Of the two instances when brothers scored centuries in the same Test match, one involved the Chappell brothers but who were the other brothers?

11. Who was the first man after World War Two to score 1,000 Test runs in a calendar year and in which year?

12. Which English cricketer was sent in as night watchman against Australia in 1932-33 and scored ninety-eight?

13. Who scored 1,000 runs in England before the end of May in 1973?

14. In the fifth England-Australia Test at Lords in 1964 Colin Cowdrey reached the milestone of his 5,000th Test run in the second innings. Which Englishman reached the milestone of his 4,000th Test run in the first innings?

15. Who scored the first double century in the Packer series of matches?

16. In the second Test between Australia and Pakistan in 1978-79, which Australian batsman became only the second in Test history to be dismissed 'handled ball'?

17. Whose only Test century for England was 214 not out against India at Edgbaston in 1974?

18. When J.H. Edrich and G. Boycott scored their 100th centuries they both had the same batting partner at the time of reaching this milestone.
    (a) Who was their partner?
    (b) In what year did this occur?

19. Which batsman scored a double century at Worcester on each of the three occasions that he played there before the Second World War?

FIFTH QUIZ: ACHIEVEMENTS

20. Where did D.G. Bradman score his 100th century and against whom?

21. In 1975 which batsman hit a century in just forty-four minutes against the Australians?

22. Who was Mike Procter playing for at the time he scored six consecutive centuries in 1970-71?

23. In 1969-70 who faced five deliveries in one over from Ashley Mallett and hit each one for six?

24. Who was the first batsman to score centuries against all six Test-playing countries, prior to Sri Lanka's inclusion?

25. (a) Who scored the only century in the 1980 India-England Golden Jubilee Test match?
    (b) Why did the Rest Day take place after one day?

26. Who was the only batsman to score a century in the 1956 Old Trafford Test in which Jim Laker claimed his nineteen victims?

27. (a) Which batsman scored his maiden first-class century in 1981, twenty years after making his first-class debut?
    (b) In 1984 who scored his maiden first-class hundred in his 380th innings?

28. (a) Who is the only England batsman to have scored a century in each innings of a Test match since World War Two, and where and when did this occur?
    (b) Who achieved the same for Australia in the same game?

29. Which man scored the only Test century at Bramall Lane?

30. When Gary Sobers scored his record 365 against Pakistan in 1957-58, which West Indian also scored a double century in the same innings?

31. Who scored over 1,000 runs on India's tour of Australia in 1947-48?

32. Who was the last Englishman to score a Test double century, before David Gower in 1979?

33. In the 1938 England-Australia Test series, which batsman had only one innings, scoring 187?

34. Who was the first woman to score a Test century at Sydney in 1934?

35. Who was the only batsman not dismissed twice by Jim Laker in the 1956 Old Trafford Test?

36. Which West Indian cricketer scored over 4,000 runs in Test cricket, yet hit only two sixes, both in the same game against Australia at Port of Spain in 1954-55?

37. Who were the four men who scored centuries for England both before and after the Second World War?

38. Which batsman has scored the most centuries for Middlesex?

39. Who was the last batsman to reach the milestone of 100 first-class centuries?

40. Who are the four batsmen to have scored 100 before lunch on the first day of a Test match?

41. Which batsman made the highest individual Test innings without a six in it?

42. (a) In 1981 who became the second batsman to score a first-class century against all seventeen first class counties?
    (b) Who was the first to do so?

43. When England scored 903 against Australia in 1938 and Hutton scored his record 364, who were the other two England batsmen who scored centuries?

44. Who scored three runs in 100 minutes for England against Australia in 1962-63?

45. Who carried her bat through England's second innings in the third Test against the West Indies in 1979 when she scored 112 out of a total 164?

Bowling

46. Who has taken most Test wickets for Australia?

47. Whose record (for all countries) did he beat?

48. When Fred Trueman became the world's most prolific Test wicket taker, whose record did he beat?

49. (a) Whose bowling shattered England at The Oval in 1882?
    (b) What legend resulted from Australia's victory?

50. Who was the first bowler to bowl 20,000 balls in a Test career?

51. Who was the Indian bowler in a Test match against England who bowled a record twenty-one consecutive maidens and, in one twenty-nine over spell in the match, bowled twenty-six maidens for three runs and no wickets?

52. Which South African took a hat trick, and four wickets in five balls, for the Rest of the World against England at Leeds in 1970?

53. Which bowler took seven for one in a spell during the Australia-Pakistan first Test in 1978-79?

54. When Derek Underwood took his 2,000th first-class wicket in 1981 who was the last man before him to reach this milestone — the man who, coincidentally, was Underwood's very first victim?

55. Who took ten for ten against Nottinghamshire in 1932?

56. Which bowler holds the record for taking the most Test wickets in a twelve-month period?

57. Which man took 100 Test wickets in sixteen, the least number, of Test matches?

58. Who took five for thirty-eight in the final of the 1979 Prudential World Cup?

59. Which side dismissed the West Indian tourists for a mere twenty-five runs in 1969?

60. Which bowler took over 1,000 first-class wickets in the 1950's and also in the 1960's?

61. Prior to Ian Botham's taking his 200th Test wicket in a record forty-one Tests in 1981, who held the record for England, which he achieved in forty-four matches?

62. Who claimed his 500th first-class victim when he dismissed Geoff Boycott in the first Test of the New Zealand-England series in 1977-78?

63. Off which bowler did Geoff Boycott score his record-

FIFTH QUIZ: ACHIEVEMENTS

breaking run in 1981/82 when he overtook Gary Sobers' record of the most Test runs?

64. Who was Fred Trueman's last Test victim and was also the last man to dismiss Trueman in Test cricket at Lords in 1965?

65. Who was the Surrey player who left the club because they would not award him a cap despite having won one for England?

66. Which England bowler in 1953-54 became the first man this century to be no-balled in a Test match for 'throwing'?

67. Who took 252 first-class wickets at 16.22 each during tours of England in 1897, 1903 and 1908?

68. Jim Laker took nineteen wickets in the 1956 Old Trafford Test, but who was the next most prolific wicket taker in the match, with four victims?

69. Don Bradman only claimed two Test victims as a bowler. In 1930-31 he dismissed the West Indies wicketkeeper, Barrow; in 1932-33 who was his other victim?

70. Who is the only man to have taken fifteen wickets in one day's play in a Test match?

71. Who had the best bowling analysis in the Prudential World Cup between 1975 and 1983?

72. Who was the first bowler after World War Two to perform the hat trick in a Test match?

73. In 1956 there were four instances of bowlers taking ten wickets in an innings. Jim Laker did it twice, Tony Lock once and who else performed this feat?

74. Who was the last bowler before Rodney Hogg in 1979 to dismiss Geoff Boycott for a duck in a Test match?

75. Who opened his Test career by bowling eight successive maiden overs, and in which Test?

76. Who took three wickets in the final over of the Australia-Scotland match in 1981?

77. Apart from Derek Underwood, who took over 100 first-class wickets in both 1978 and 1979?

78. Derek Underwood took nine for thirty-two in an innings against Surrey in the 1978 County Championship. Prior to this who was the last bowler to take nine in an innings?

79. Which cricketer knocked the bat out of Don Bradman's hands with his fourth delivery, and had him caught with his fifth?

Wicketkeeping

80. Following Rodney Marsh's defection to the Packer circus, who took over as Australia's wicketkeeper initially?

81. Which ex-wicketkeeper managed the 1984 West Indies touring team to England?

82. Two of the six wicketkeepers who have claimed over 1,000 first-class victims have the same surname — what is it?

83. Who took 656 catches and made 344 stumpings between 1921 and 1947, to finish with a career record of exactly 1,000 dismissals?

FIFTH QUIZ: ACHIEVEMENTS 65

84. Who scored two Test centuries for England (104 on both occasions), the first against the West Indies at Old Trafford in 1950 and the second against India at Lords in 1952?

85. In the Test at Lords in 1956 who became the first wicketkeeper to dismiss nine batsmen in a Test?

86. When Derek Randall made his debut for England in 1976-77 against India, which wicketkeeper made his debut for England in the same match although not as a wicketkeeper?

87. Who took an all-time record of ninety-six catches in a season in 1960?

88. Which wicketkeeper has achieved the target of 200 Test victims in the least number of matches?

89. Who made fourteen stumpings in fourteen matches on an Australian tour of England?

90. Which wicketkeeper in 1981 became only the third since World War Two to score a century in each innings in a first-class match?

91. Which Tasmanian made two triple hundreds in minor cricket, scored forty-one runs in two Tests and toured England in 1890, selected partly because J.M. Blackham thought, erroneously, that he was a wicketkeeper?

92. Who set a new record for New Zealand by dismissing twenty-three South Africans in the 1961-62 series?

93. Who was the wicketkeeper who established a world record in 1964 by catching eleven batsmen in one match?

94. Who was the England wicketkeeper who conceded a record thirty-seven byes in a Test innings against Australia at the Oval in 1934?

First and Last

95. Who was the first man to score 30 Test hundreds?

96. In 1963 at the age of eighteen who became the youngest bowler to take 100 wickets in his debut season?

97. In 1979 who became the first Australian to score over 1,000 Test runs in his first Test year?

98. Who was the first all-rounder to do the double in an English season?

99. Which Queensland Test bowler scored his maiden first-class 100 a few weeks before his retirement in 1982?

100. Who was the last batsman to score 1,000 first-class runs in May?

101. Who made his debut for Western Australia against the MCC in December 1977 and, after just eight first-class matches, played for Australia against India in January 1978?

102. Who was the first man to reach the milestone of scoring 100 first-class centuries?

103. Who was the first Australian bowler to take more than 200 Test wickets?

104. Who was the last Englishman to carry his bat through a Test innings?

105. Who was called up to play for Australia in the Old Trafford Test in 1981, after only six first-class matches?

106. What was the outcome of D.K. Lillee's last ball in Test cricket?

107. Basil Williams scored a century on his Test debut for the West Indies against Australia in 1978, but which other West Indian scored his maiden Test century in the same match?

108. (a) Who was the last man to score 300 runs in a Test innings?
 (b) Where and against whom?

109. Who gained selection for Australia to tour England in 1961 after only eleven first-class matches?

110. Who is the oldest cricketer to have made his debut in a Test match for Australia?

111. Two uncapped players were in the England party to tour Australia and India in 1979-80. One was Graham Dilley but who was the other?

112. Which Pakistan bowler took the wicket of Australian Colin MacDonald with the first ball he bowled in Test cricket?

113. Who was the first batsman to score a Test century?

114. Which bowler in his maiden Test match took eight for eighty-four in the first innings and eight for fifty-three in the second?

115. In 1978 who became the first Indian batsman to have scored a Test century against all other Test countries that India had played?

116. (a) Who was the last man to score a century and double century in the same Test match?
(b) When and against whom?

117. Lawrence Rowe is one of the only two men to have scored 300 runs or more in their first Test match: who is the other?

118. Who was the last batsman to reach the milestone of 50,000 first-class runs?

119. Who was captain of Sri Lanka in its first official Test?

120. Who was the first Sri Lankan batsman to score centuries in both innings of a Test?

121. In 1969 who became the first New Zealand bowler to take 100 Test wickets?

122. Which Leicestershire bowler was the first to register a hat trick in the Benson & Hedges Cup when he did so in 1972?

123. Who was the Test Cricketer who was first dismissed by Tony Lock and last dismissed by Derek Underwood?

124. Sunil Gavaskar was Ian Botham's 100th Test victim in 1979: who was his first in 1977?

125. Who were the three batsmen who scored centuries against England in 1980 during their first appearance in a Lords Test match?

126. Who was the Australian batsman who became the first to score a century in each innings in a Test match?

127. In England's first post-war Test match against India in 1946, who were the only two debutants in the home side?

FIFTH QUIZ: ACHIEVEMENTS

128. In the Old Trafford Test of 1976, who dismissed Roy Fredericks, Viv Richards and Alvin Kallicharran in his first three and a half overs in Test cricket?

129. Who was the bowler who made his debut for Australia the same day as Geoff Boycott made his debut for England, and was also the first man to dismiss Boycott in Test cricket?

130. Eric Hollies was the last man to dismiss Don Bradman in a Test match: who was the first?

131. Who was the last South African to score a century in a Test match for South Africa?

132. Who played his seventy-ninth and last game for England the day they dismissed New Zealand for twenty-six, the lowest ever Test score?

133. Who made his Test debut for Australia on the same day as Don Bradman?

134. Who was the last England bowler to claim a victim with his first ball in Test cricket?

135. Which Englishman, after World War Two, scored his maiden first-class century on his Test debut?

136. In 1980 who became the first man since Arnold Dyson in 1937 to score a century before lunch on the first day of the season?

The One-Day Game
137. Sri Lanka was one of the two non Test-playing countries which took part in the final stages of the 1979 Prudential World Cup. Which was the other?

138. Who won the man of the match award in the 1979 Prudential World Cup final?

139. When Australia scored 302 for eight against New Zealand in the 1982-83 Benson & Hedges World Series second final match, who scored 117?

140. Who took six for fifteen for Yorkshire in a Gillette Cup match against Somerset in 1965?

141. For which country did father and son, Carstein and Claud Morild, play in the 1979 Prudential World Cup?

142. Which Australian bowler took five for twenty-one against Canada in the 1979 World Cup in England?

143. Who at the age of seventeen, was the youngest member of any of the 1983 World Cup squads?

144. In the 1982-83 Benson & Hedges World Series, of the four centuries scored for England, David Gower made three but who made the other?

145. Who was the sixteen-year-old who performed the hat trick in a John Player League game against Derbyshire in 1982 in his second John Player League game?

146. Who is the only player to have scored a century before lunch in a Prudential World Cup game?

147. In the 1979-80 Benson & Hedges World Series finals when the West Indies beat England two-nil, which player scored eighty and ninety-eight in the two games?

148. In 1982 who became the first man to score 6,000 runs in the John Player League?

149. Who has made the highest individual score for Australia

FIFTH QUIZ: ACHIEVEMENTS 71

in a Prudential World Cup game?

150. Who is the only man who has won man of the match awards in two Gillette Cup finals?

151. Who took six wickets for nine runs in a John Player League game against Derbyshire in 1979?

152. Which was the first minor county to reach the third round of the Gillette Cup?

153. In the game when Trevor Chappell bowled the last ball underarm, which New Zealand player had given his side a chance of victory with 102 not out?

154. Who is the only Pakistan player to score a century in a Benson & Hedges World Series game?

155. Which is the only county to have won the County Championship, Gillette Cup, John Player League and the Benson & Hedges Cup?

156. Durham was the first minor county to beat a first-class county in the Gillette Cup: which was the second?

157. When England picked two players for their 1979 Prudential World Cup squad who had not toured Australia the previous winter, Wayne Larkins was one, but who was the other?

158. During the 1979-80 Benson & Hedges World Series group games who was the only Englishman to score a century?

159. Which country did Chris Chappell play for in the 1979 Prudential World Cup?

160. When playing against Essex in a John Player League

game in 1969 who bowled eight overs, eight maidens and took none for none?

161. Which batsman has made the highest score, 158, in a Benson & Hedges World Series game?

162. In 1977 Barry Wood became the first Lancashire player to score 1,000 runs and take 100 wickets in the John Player League. Who, later the same season, became the second Lancashire player to perform the feat?

163. Which is the only county to have appeared in the semi-final of the Gillette Cup four years in succession?

164. Who was the first cricketer, in 1981, to be recalled to the wicket after being dismissed in the Benson & Hedges Cup when it was found that the fielding side had only five players rather than six inside the new experimental thirty-yard circle?

165. Sussex won the 1982 John Player League with a record fifty-eight points, beating the old record of fifty-four, set by which team?

166. In 1980 who became only the third man to score 1,000 John Player League runs with two different counties and, in doing so, performed the feat against his old county?

167. Which county finished runners-up in the John Player League in 1971, 1976 and 1977?

168. For whom did Brian Close appear in a final at Lords in 1979?

Captains
169. Who was captain of the West Indies side in the tied Test

match of 1960-61?

170. Who was captain of the Australian side?

171. Who was the England captain who scored his only Test century against India in 1972-73?

172. Who was the last England captain before Mike Brearley, in 1978-79, to win four Tests in Australia in one series?

173. Who was captain when Australia won back the Ashes in 1934?

174. Who was the first Leicestershire player to captain England in a Test match?

175. Who captained Australia in the Centenary Test Match against England in 1977?

176. In the 1964 England-Australia Test at Old Trafford both captains scored centuries: one was Bobby Simpson but who was the other?

177. Which player had been in first-class cricket for the shortest period before taking over captaincy of the English Test side?

178. Which Yorkshireman scored 160 not out when captaining England under-nineteens against the West Indies under-nineteens in 1978?

179. Who was the first man to have captained Australia in a Test match before he had captained his state?

180. Who captained India, having previously played for England?

181. Who was Pakistan's first Test captain?

182. Name each of the last two men to captain an England side which included a member of the team who was his own county captain?

183. Which England captain has scored the highest individual Test innings whilst captain?

184. Who led a national team to tour another country while there was a war going on between the peoples of each?

185. Whose record did Bobby Simpson beat when he captained Australia for a record thirty-first time in the second Test with India in 1977-78?

186. Who was the player who never captained England but took over the captaincy of the team on the fifth day of the fourth Test against Australia in 1950-51?

187. Who captained Australia in South Africa in 1935-36?

188. Geoff Boycott has opened the England batting with three men who have captained England — Brearley, Edrich and who else?

189. Who were the father and son who both captained England?

190. Who captained Pakistan in the 1979 Prudential World Cup?

191. Who was captain of the Indian side which beat England in 1971, the first time India had beaten England in England?

192. In the 1968 England-Australia series, who captained England and Australia in the fourth Test at Leeds?

193. (a) Who caused controversy in a Benson & Hedges Cup

FIFTH QUIZ: ACHIEVEMENTS 75

iv What did these spectators at Lord's have so much to cheer about?

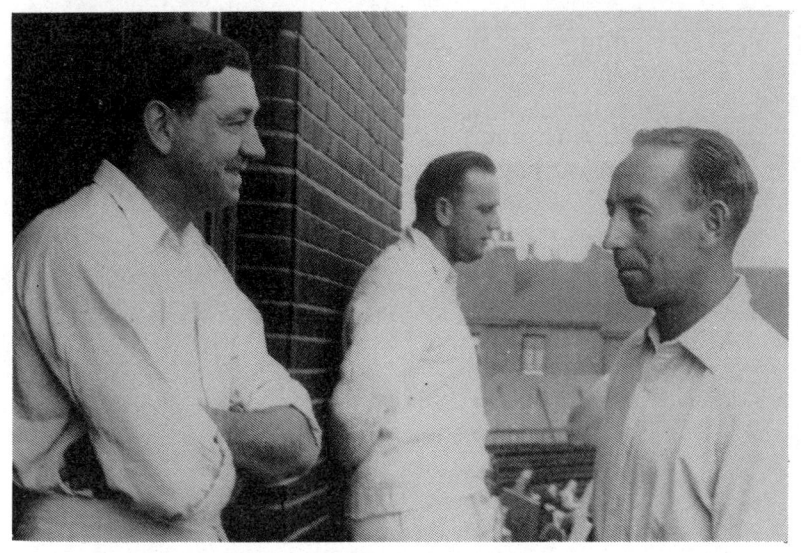

v   Who are these two captains sharing a word before the match?

tie in 1979 when he declared after only one over at one for nought?
(b) What were the consequences of his action?

194. Who was South Africa's captain the last time they toured England, in 1965?

195. Which man has scored the highest individual innings in a Test match in which he was captain?

196. Which captain won the toss in all five Tests in a Test series in 1966 and in another Test series in 1971-72?

197. Who was the Northants skipper who led his side to victory in the 1980 Benson & Hedges Cup final?

198. Who was Ireland's captain for their first ever Gillette Cup match in 1980?

199. Which county captain of the 1980s was born in West Germany?

200. (a) Which Australian player, when no-balled while bowling at England's captain in a Test, deliberately threw the next ball at him?
(b) Who was the batsman?

SIXTH QUIZ
ALL-ROUNDERS IN OTHER FIELDS

1. Which man's first job after leaving school was as a clerk in a Basingstoke mental hospital? He then joined the Hampshire constabulary in 1934, but resigned to join the BBC in 1945.

2. Name the post-war Australian opening bat whose hobby was racing pigeons — the birds going somewhat faster than his scoring rate.

3. Which post-war West Indian batsman became a practising member of the 'Moral Re-armament Movement' in the 1960's, and still is?

4. Which well-known cricketer once held the World long-jump record?

5. Which post-war 'scourge' of Australian cricket emigrated there to become a schoolmaster, but gave up the teaching profession to become the chief cricket coach in Victoria?

6. Don Bradman, apart from being an excellent cricketer and fine golfer, also excelled in another sport, winning the South Australian title. What was his other sport?

7. Which former Australian bowler settled in England in the late 1880's and became a Director of the 'Star Tea Company'?

8. What, apart from cricket, did Jack Fingleton write about in Australian newspapers?

9. Who are the only two people to have represented England at both cricket and full international soccer level since the Second World War?

10. Who was born in 1921, an Australian batsman and occasional bowler, and became a member of the Australian Parliament as a Liberal-Country MP?

11. Which Australian cricketer, later a Lancashire captain, also played soccer and basketball for New South Wales?

12. Which England wicketkeeper obtained a Bachelor of Law degree at Exeter University?

13. Which England Test player had his hair cut 1920's style so as to appear in a film in 1980?

14. Which Australian batsman of the 1960's had previously represented Australia at hockey in the 1956 Olympic Games, and is now a teacher and Anglican lay reader, involving himself in community welfare projects?

15. Which post-war England cricketer won an FA Amateur Cup winners medal with Walthamstow Avenue in 1952?

16. Name an Australian leg-spinner who later became a journalist and was also a skilful artist.

17. Which Commonwealth Prime Minister, during his period as Lord Warden of the Cinque Ports, paid regular visits to Canterbury Week and was elected President of Kent in 1969?

18. For which West Indian fast bowler are fast projectiles not unfamiliar as he is also a qualified air traffic controller?

19. Who was the nineteenth-century Yorkshire cricketer,

with the same name as a British Prime Minister, who was sacked by his county in 1897 after he came on the field under the influence of alcohol, and 'misbehaved' himself on the pitch?

20. Which Australian Test captain married three times and fathered sixteen children?

21. Who was the last England captain to represent his country at Rugby Union?

22. Who was the post-war England captain who went on to become a popular BBC radio broadcaster, after demonstrating his all round athleticism by being North of England squash champion six times and winning blues for hockey and Rugby fives?

23. Which West Indian Test captain of the 1930's went as a missionary to Africa when his career finished?

24. Who studied Sociology at Manchester University prior to being appointed Warden of the University College of the West Indies?

25. Who was the successful post-war South African cricket captain who became an influential medical consultant in Johannesburg?

26. Which player has captained a winning FA Cup final team at Wembley since the war, played soccer for his country, and also represented his country at cricket?

27. Who is the only man to have enjoyed the following distinctions:
    (a) played Test cricket for England
    (b) played in a County Championship winning side
    (c) won an FA Cup Winners medal
    (d) played in a football league championship winning team, and

(e) played for England at soccer?

28. Which South African fast bowler, signed by Northamptonshire in 1984, is a noted landscape artist?

29. Which Middlesex and England batsman is a devout member of the Anglican church and works for the Inter-Action Group in deprived areas of London?

30. Which opening batsman was capped for England at both soccer and cricket in the 1950's, and on his retirement pursued a full-time interest in greyhound racing — much to the detriment of the 'bookies'?

31. Which Australian batsman was left out of the England tour in 1972, so came over to teach at Charterhouse, partly to pursue his hobby of fishing? He is now in business as an antique dealer, and active in politics.

32. Which England batsman of the 1930's died of a heart attack in 1952 while playing polo?

33. What was the name of the well-known English actor and Test cricketer who went to live in Hollywood in the 1920's, where his well known love of cricket was typified by his revitalising the game in the United States? He was knighted for his services to Anglo-American friendship.

34. Who was the post-war English fast bowler who became a very successful City businessman, a Steward of the Jockey Club, and also acted as Australia's representative on the ICC?

35. Which Australian captain practised medicine and was renowned as a Greek scholar? What was his nickname?

36. Who is the only person to have captained England at both soccer and cricket?

SIXTH QUIZ: ALL-ROUNDERS IN OTHER FIELDS 81

37. Name the Australian batsman of the 1960's and 1970's who was a brilliant fielder and now teaches mathematics in Australia?

38. Name the former England Test captain who, after many attempts, eventually won the Oxford and Cambridge Universities 'Presidents Putter' golf competition in 1983?

39. Who was the South African Test cricketer who played Rugby Union for England and was regarded as one of the world's finest centre-threequarters in the immediate post-war era?

40. Which Australian Test batsman became executive director of the Australian Lawn Tennis Association?

41. Which Pakistani became the first cricketer to appear in the first-class game while on bail for alleged political activities, doing so in the 1968-69 season?

42. Who was the long-serving Hampshire batsman who ran a sports shop in Southampton and a public house near Bournemouth before tragically losing his sight?

43. Name the unfortunate England captain who emigrated to South Africa and set up in partnership in the motor trade. However, he lost all his money when his partner, of the 'Arfur Daley' ilk, ran off with it.

44. Who is the only England Test cricketer ever to have won an Olympic Boxing gold medal?

45. At what sport, other than cricket, was Colin Cowdrey a champion?

46. Which Australian all-rounder played for Oxford, Middlesex and the Gentlemen, also won golf and rugby

i One of Barbados' top golfers. Why will he remember ten hours in 1957?

blues, became Australian Amateur Golf Champion, and was an ear, nose and throat specialist?

47. Who was the last Oxbridge undergraduate to score a Test century for England?

48. Name the former Hearts and Scotland soccer player who was in the Scotland squad that took part in the 1980 Benson & Hedges Cup?

49. Rick Charlesworth, a recent captain of Western Australia, was Australia's captain in what World Championships of 1979 — in which they reached the final?

50. Which former England fast bowler used to play saxophone in a jazz band at the Savoy Hotel in the 1920's?

SEVENTH QUIZ
DOMESTIC COMPETITIONS

A. England

1. (a) Which was the last county to join the County Championship?
   (b) When?

2. Which first-class county has the Prince of Wales' feathers on its badge?

3. Which was the last side to win the County Championship three years in succession?

4. For which first-class county other than Surrey did Jim Laker play?

5. . . . and Surrey's Tony Lock played for which other first-class county?

6. Who captained Yorkshire between 1933 and 1947, and in the nine seasons he was in charge led the county to six Championship wins?

7. Who was the last Middlesex bowler before Mike Selvey in 1978, to take 100 wickets in a first-class season?

8. Who was the last bowler to take 200 wickets in a first-class season?

9. When Surrey won the County Championship seven times between 1952 and 1958, which county finished runners-up to them three times?

10. Who was the last man to win the Young Cricketer of the Year award and play in a Championship winning team in the same year?

11. Who captained Essex to their first ever County Championship win in 1979, in the deciding game?

12. Name the two sides that umpire 'Dickie' Bird played County cricket for.

13. Essex, in 1979, won the County Championship for the first time — which was the last county before them to win it for the first time?

14. Who was the last man before Bill Alley to score 3,000 runs in a first-class season?

15. Which is the only first-class county to have established its record score since the war?

16. Who scored a century in a 'Roses' match in each of the four seasons between 1979 and 1982?

17. Who, in scoring 248 at Lords in 1981, scored the highest individual innings on the ground for 33 years?

18. Who, in 1972, was the last bowler to take four wickets in four balls in a County Championship match?

19. Name the two men to have played County Championship cricket in five decades.

20. Who in 1982, became only the third number eleven batsman to score a century in the history of the County Championship?

21. Which bowler took nine for twelve in a County Championship match in 1958?

22. Which player in 1982 became only the second ever to appear in the County Championship for a fourth different county?

SEVENTH QUIZ: DOMESTIC COMPETITIONS

23. Whom did Jack Bond succeed as captain of Lancashire?

24. David Steele joined a small band of players to re-join their former county when he went back to Northants. Who was the last man before Steele to return to a former county?

25. The highest individual innings for Nottinghamshire was one of 312 not out by WW Keeton at the Oval in 1939. Who were Notts playing at the time?

26. Who performed the hat trick on the opening day of the 1978 season, and on the final day took one wicket to end the season with exactly 100?

27. Since the re-structuring of the County Championship in 1969, who was the first man to score 2,000 runs in a season?

28. Which fellow Kent player is the brother-in-law of Graham Dilley?

29. Name the two counties Geoff Pullar played for in the County Championship.

30. Who succeeded Ray Illingworth as Leicestershire captain in 1979?

31. Allan Border, Australian Test cricketer, played Lancashire League cricket in England. Which first-class county did he also play *one game* for?

32. Name the two teams involved in the last 'tied' game in the County Championship.

33. Kerry O'Keeffe, the Australian cricketer, played first-class cricket in England in 1971 and 1972 for which county?

34. Which side in a County Championship match in 1979 declared at 146 for six, but then realised they had their sums 'all wrong' — and had to follow on?

35. Which man scored a century on his first-class debut in the 1978 County Championship?

36. Which Glamorgan player hit a century before lunch — in just sixty-one balls against Surrey in 1976?

37. Emrys Davies in 1937 was the last man before Mike Procter to perform what feat?

38. Mike Brearley's father played first-class cricket, albeit only three matches: two of those three were for Middlesex, and the third was against Middlesex — who was he playing for on that occasion?

39. Name the county which fielded a side including ten Test players in a County Championship match against Leicestershire in August 1972. And for a bonus point — name the only 'uncapped' player in their side.

40. Name the three counties since the last war who have gone through a season of County Championship matches without a win.

41. Who was left out of the England team for the Centenary Test in 1980, but played for his county instead and returned career-best figures of eight for 57, perhaps deprived of all ten by Northants' declaration at 200-8?

42. In the same match in which Glenn Turner scored his maiden first-class triple century in 1982, which other batsman was scoring his maiden first-class double century?

43. Which firm sponsors the monthly and annual awards made to wicketkeepers in England each year?

44. Name the Australian bowler who played for Middlesex in the 1969 and 1970 seasons.

. . . and now for a trip around some grounds!

45. Which is the most northerly ground in England upon which first-class County cricket is played?

46. Which famous Test ground is the home of the William Ansell stand?

47. The St Lawrence ground is the home of which first-class county?

48. If you were drinking at the 'Jessop Tavern', at which ground would you be?

49. Which cricket ground once had the Mumbles railway passing outside its gates?

50. Where would you be watching County cricket if you were at the Mote?

51. Which county do you associate with the Wagon Works Ground?

B. Australia

52. (a) Which state holds the distinction of recording the highest completed innings in the Sheffield Shield, and
    (b) Who has scored the lowest?

53. For which state did England Test cricketer Colin Milburn play in the Sheffield Shield?

54. Which Australian in 1982 hit a century in the least number of balls in first-class cricket — just thirty-nine?

55. Who succeeded Geoff Boycott as captain of Australian side Waverley in 1977-78?

56. Name the three states that contested the first ever Sheffield Shield competition.

57. Which team won the Sheffield Shield each year from 1953-54 until 1961-62 inclusive?

58. Who partnered Derek Chadwick in a Western Australia first wicket record in 1968-69?

59. Which player took part in twenty-two century partnerships with Bill Ponsford?

60. Which player has scored most first-class runs for South Australia in the Sheffield Shield?

61. Which bowler has taken most first-class wickets for Queensland?

62. Who took a hat trick when bowling for South Australia against MCC at Adelaide in 1935-36?

63. Who is the only Australian bowler to take four wickets in four balls in a first-class game in Australia?

64. Which Australian bowler has taken most first-class wickets in a career?

65. On which ground did Bradman score his 452 against Queensland in 1929-30?

66. To whom is the Belvidere Cup awarded?

67. Which batsman broke Sir Donald Bradman's record for the most runs scored in the Sheffield Shield?

SEVENTH QUIZ: DOMESTIC COMPETITIONS

68. The 'Gabba' is the home of Test cricket in Brisbane. On what other ground in Brisbane has Test cricket been played?

69. Outside which ground is the Gloucester Park Trotting Track?

70. Which Australia all-rounder was known as the 'WG of Australia'?

71. Who was the fellow County cricketer who succeeded Jack Simmons as Captain of Tasmania for the 1980-81 Sheffield Shield competition?

72. Who was the first cricketer — in 1978 — to receive the Membership of the Order of Australia?

73. Who was the first bowler to take 100 wickets in an Australian season?

74. Who has scored most Sheffield Shield runs for New South Wales?

75. Who was the first man to score six centuries in one Sheffield Shield season?

76. Who was the first Tasmanian-born batsman to score a century for Tasmania in the Sheffield Shield?

77. Which Australian Test wicketkeeper once claimed twelve New South Wales victims in one match whilst he was playing for Queensland?

C. Around the World

78. After whom is India's Ranji Trophy named?

79. Who were the first winners of the West Indian Shell Shield in 1965-66?

80. Who was the first man to reach the milestone of 500 runs in Plunkett Shield matches in New Zealand in one season?

81. If you were watching first-class cricket at the Kensington Oval, in which country would you be?

82. Which side won India's Ranji Trophy every year from 1959 to 1973?

83. By what name is the South African state Kimberley now known?

84. What is the name of the principal domestic competition in Pakistan?

85. The West Indian Shell Shield was first contested in 1965-66: name the five sides that took part.

86. While still attending Otago High School, who made his first-class debut in New Zealand in December 1964?

87. Name the only three Provinces who won the Currie Cup in South Africa between 1892 and 1970.

88. Who is credited with the first century in the West Indian Shell Shield?

89. And who scored the first century?

90. Who was the first man to score two triple centuries in New Zealand's Plunkett Shield?

91. Which player, in scoring an undefeated eighty-two runs for Eastern Province in the Currie Cup, became the top run-maker of all time in the competition, when he took his total to 6,835 runs?

SEVENTH QUIZ: DOMESTIC COMPETITIONS 93

92. In which country can the Trafalgar Park ground be found?

93. And in which country is the Kent Park ground?

94. The Plunkett Shield was first contested in New Zealand in 1907, but it was not until 1921-22 that its present league format was adopted. Who were the first winners under the 'league' system?

95. Which player, playing in his first West Indian Shell Shield tournament in 1967-68, established a new record for the competition with an innings of 205, and also set a new bowling record for the competition with seven for 124?

i   A Gillette Cup winning team. What team is it, when did they win and who are all the players?

96. Which man scored 846 runs for an amazing average of 169.20 in the 1936-37 Currie Cup?

97. The Currie Cup batting record was broken twice within five days in the 1950-51 competition. Name the two batsman who scored 271 not out and 277 not out respectively?

98. Why did the 1944-45 final of the Ranji Trophy attract a crowd of 40,000?

99. Which man, in 1979, scored 490 runs for Ireland — a record for the country in one season?

100. In which country is the Euratom Varese Club a leading cricket team?

EIGHTH QUIZ
ART AND LITERATURE

1. Who wrote *Tales from a Long Room?*

2. Which humorist and playwright brought out a book in 1981 at the age of ninety-four entitled *94 declared: Cricket Reminiscences?*

3. Who wrote *Sir Donald Bradman — a Biography*, published in 1978 to coincide with the great man's seventieth birthday?

4. Where were the English cricketers bound on board the 'Nova Scotian' from Liverpool in 1859?

5. Who was founder and first editor of the current Australian *Cricketer?*

6. Who was the prolific and respected writer who died just two days short of his seventy-seventh birthday in July 1982?

7. Whose autobiography was entitled *Sort of a Cricket Person?*

8. Who painted *Lords Cricket Ground. England v Australia, 1938?*

9. Who is an Indian-born biographer of Keith Miller?

10. Who were the illustrators of *The Lords Taverners Fifty Greatest?*

11. Who published an autobiography entitled *Over to Me* containing outspoken comments which resulted in his

being sacked by his county Cricket Club? (He is now a member of the committee).

12. Who was the author of *With Bat and Ball* (Ward Lock, 1898) who was known as 'the W.G. of Australia'?

13. Who wrote *Days in the Sun*?

14. What was the title of the Australian edition of *The Glad Season* by Ray Robinson which was published under this title in England in 1955?

15. Which two British cricket authors had 'Wallah' in their titles?

16. Which fictitious Sussex club is immortalised in *The Cricket Match* by Hugh de Selincourt?

17. How old was Colin Cowdrey when his *A Time for Reflection* was published?

18. Which former England captain entitled his first autobiography *From Verse to Worse*?

19. Who was, according to Sir Pelham Warner, 'The Herodotus of Cricket'?

20. When Hugh de Selincourt's 'Paul Gauvinier' retired from cricket, to which sport did he turn?

21. Who wrote the following: "I imagine that the Lord one day gathered together a heap of Yorkshire clay and breathed into it and said 'Emmott Robinson, go on and bowl at the pavilion end for Yorkshire'."?

22. What was the title of Jack Fingleton's first book?

23. Who wrote of seeing soldiers:
"in foul dug-outs, gnawed by rats,

And in the ruined trenches, lashed with rain,
Dreaming of things they did with balls and bats"?

24. Who wrote and in which book: "Meanwhile, Tavaré kept going with his vital innings, tortoise to Botham's hare... 'I like batting with Tav' said Ian afterwards. 'He seems to understand my calls even when I mean the opposite.' Later christened 'Rowdy' in India, because he talks so little, Tavaré is a good listener, and when he says no he means it."?

25. Who painted a vast picture of F.S. Trueman?

26. Which cricketer is best remembered for his *History of Cricket*, first published in book form in 1926? (He was also a great authority on Winchester Cathedral)

27. Under what *nom de plume* did the Rev. R.L. Hodgson write?

28. Who illustrated *A Cricket Bag* by James Thorpe?

29. (a) Former Kent cricketer, musician, classical scholar, writer and artist, Nicholas Wanostrocht was better known by a much simpler name — what was it?
    (b) What cricketing aid did he invent?

30. Who wrote *The Cricket Field*?

31. Who edited *The Hambledon Men*?

32. About which Test series did Jack Fingleton write *Four Chukkas to Australia*?

33. What are the initials and surname of the amateur cricketer-cracksman created by E.W. Hornung?

34. Who is the subject of *The Perfect Batsman* by

A.C. MacLaren?

35. Whose 'Uncle Walter' is quoted at regular intervals in his books?

36. Who was the County cricket historian killed in the Munich air disaster of 1958, involving Manchester United F.C.?

37. Who was the first winner (1970) of The Cricket Society's Silver Jubilee Literary Award?

38. Which ships' companies are depicted playing at latitude 69.22°N., March 1823?

39. Who wrote, where and of whom:
"As he walked past me he smiled, patted the back of his bat and said, 'It was too good for me'. There was no triumph in me as I watched the receding figure. I felt like a boy who had killed a dove."?

40. Who were (a) Old Ebor, (b) Tityrus, (c) John Marchant, and (d) Gryllus?

41. Which England bowler, who died on active service in the Second World War, had his autobiography published in 1940?

42. Name the compilers and editors of *Wisden's Cricketers' Almanack* since its inception in 1864?

43. Who founded and captained (a) Allahakbarries, (b) Invalids, and (c) Heartaches?

44. Who were the three cricket-loving brothers who each had a book published in 1949?

45. Who wrote the following and where: "Bradman was one

of the most curious mixtures of good and bad batting I have ever seen... Promise there is in Bradman in plenty, though watching him does not inspire one with any confidence that he desires to take the only course which will lead him to a fulfilment of that promise."?

46. Who played for Oxford University, Somerset and the Gentlemen, and in his first book includes "O.E. Jugg: A Memoir"?

47. Who wrote *Spedague's Dropper*?

48. Who wrote the first book-length history of Lords and MCC?

49. Who wrote, where and of which contemporary player: "A talented, erratic, fair curly-haired West Australian right-hand batsman, brilliant fieldsman in any position, traditional cricket loyalist, and sometimes Australian cricket captain."?

50. Who painted the *XI Women of Hampshire playing XI Women of Surrey at Ball's Pond, Newington*?

51. Who subtitled his first cricket book *An Anatomy of Cricketomania* and under which title?

52. Who was the first major historian of Australian cricket?

53. Which is the only book yet published about cricket songs?

54. Who wrote George Hele's biography, *Bodyline Umpire*?

55. Who wrote:
"Willow and cane, nothing but that —
O, but it's glorious, swinging the bat!
Leather and thread, there you have all —

O, but it's glorious, gripping the ball!
Grass at our feet, and the sun overhead,
Here let us play till the evening is red.
Then to our dinner, and lustily sing,
Cricket's the King of Games, Cricket is King."?

56. Who wrote:
"When Surrey ladled out defeat,
   Who did it?
When Notts and Yorks and Kent were beat,
   Who did it?
Lohmann did — George Lohmann —
   Something like a yeoman,
Neither fast nor slow man,
   George!"?

57. Who wrote:
"So let me go whate'er befall,
   And I will make a score;
I should not love thee, dear, at all,
   Loved I not batting more."?

58. Who wrote of cricket: "You do well to love it, for it is more free from anything sordid, anything dishonourable, than any game in the world. To play it keenly, honourably, generously, self-sacrificingly, is a moral lesson in itself, and the classroom is God's air and sunshine.

59. Who wrote: "I once said that through all eternity I wished no greater bliss than to watch a never-ending series of first-class matches."?

60. Who wrote and in which book: "Verity had the look and carriage of a man likely to do supremely well something that would need time and trouble. . . There was no 'breaking-point' with Verity; and his last reported words: 'keep going', were but a text on his short and splendid life."?

EIGHTH QUIZ: ART AND LITERATURE 101

i   Who painted this picture of the legendary W.G. Grace?

NINTH QUIZ

BROADCASTING AND JOURNALISTS

1. Whose last Test match commentary was made at the Centenary Test at The Oval in 1980?

2. Whom did Bill Frindall succeed as the BBC radio team's scorer?

3. In which country was the first ever broadcast of a cricket commentary in 1925?

4. ... and who was the commentator on that occasion?

5. Which broadcaster, commentating on the wedding between Prince Charles and Diana, Princess of Wales, said as the couple emerged from St Paul's Cathedral "there they come now, the happy couple, down the steps of the pavilion"?

6. Who used to say to whom: "what to you think Arthur?"?

7. Who was suspended by Channel Nine's boss, Kerry Packer, for bad language inadvertently spoken on the air?

8. What relationship was there between the two people in the answers to the last two questions?

9. Why might a well-known New Zealand sports broadcaster be mistaken for one of the Goons?

10. Who is the current BBC television Test match scorer?

11. Who is the current first-class cricketer whose father wrote a modern version of De Selincourt's *The Cricket Match* and was also a one-time Sports Editor of ITN?

12. When the BBC first started their ball-by-ball Test match coverage in 1948, who accompanied John Arlott in the commentary box?

13. Which West Indian cricket broadcaster was also a Test all-rounder and a Test umpire?

14. Who was accused of being wary of playing West Indies fast bowlers again after his television criticisms of them in 1979-80?

15. What is the connection between St Bruno tobacco and Qualcast mowing machines?

16. Which Australian cricket commentator became a well-known political commentator in England?

17. Which visiting commentator became famous in Australia for his descriptions of seagulls?

18. Which South African fast bowler became a popular radio commentator?

19. Which Australian Test batsman, dropped from the team after the first Test against England in 1932-33, spent the rest of the series giving daily ten-minute reports to the BBC?

20. The first broadcast of a cricket commentary in Britain was at Leyton on 14 May 1927. Who was the broadcaster on the Essex-New Zealand match?

21. The first cricket match to be televised in Britain was the second Test against Australia at Lords in 1938: who was the commentator?

NINTH QUIZ: BROADCASTING AND JOURNALISTS 105

22. Which England bowler and cricket writer was recorded in the scorebook of an official MCC tour "Absent bathing, 0"?

23. Who retired in 1984 after fourteen years as Editor of *The Journal of The Cricket Society*?

24. Who was the first Press representative to visit Australia with an England team?

25. Who hit eleven sixes in an innings of 135 in the last match of the 1953 Australian tour of England?

i Why is this man surrounded by journalists and what role in the drama was played by the famous TV commentator in the background?

TENTH QUIZ
RECORDS

1. When a world record score for an individual innings was established in 1959 which batsman scored 499 runs?

2. Who holds the record for the highest individual Test score?

3. Whose record did he beat?

4. Which two countries played a Test record of thirteen consecutive Test 'draws'?

5. Who has scored most Test runs for New Zealand?

6. Who was the last Englishman to score a Test triple century?

7. Who was the last Australian to score a Test triple century?

8. Who is the only man to have scored two double hundreds in the same first-class match?

9. Who holds the record for registering the highest individual Test innings at four different Test centres?

10. Which batsman, with thirty-seven, holds the record for scoring the most double centuries in first class cricket?

11. Which batsman, with a score of 336 not out, holds the record score in an individual innings by an English batsman on foreign soil?

12. Up to 1984 which player holds the record for scoring the

most Test runs in a twelve month period (not necessarily in a calendar year)?

13. In a County Championship match in 1977 who scored a world record 83.43 per cent of his team's total, when scoring 141 of the total of 169?

14. Who is the youngest person to have reached the milestone of 1,000 Test runs?

15. When he scored a century in each innings against England in 1977-78 Geoff Howarth became only the second New Zealand player to perform such a feat in a Test match. Who was the first?

16. Which batsman scored the most runs in aggregate in the Kerry Packer 'Tests'?

17. Which country had a record number of extras added to their total in a Test match, when sixty-eight were added to their total of 291?

18. Which player scored a century and a double century on his Test debut?

19. Who has performed the double of 1,000 runs and 100 wickets in a season on the greatest number of occasions?

20. Which man holds the record for scoring a century for England in the least number of balls (only seventy-five)?

21. Which Australian holds the record for the fastest ever Test century?

22. Who is the only man who has scored 400 runs in a first-class match on two occasions?

23. Whose record did Ian Botham beat when he established

the record for achieving the Test double of 1,000 runs and 100 wickets in the least number of matches?

24. Gary Sobers is the only man to have hit six sixes in one over in the County Championship, but who has scored five in an over on two occasions?

25. Which batsman holds the record for hitting the highest score on his Test debut?

26. Who shared the highest partnership for any wicket in any first-class match?

27. Who is the only man to have scored a century in each innings of a Test match on at least three occasions?

28. When Kapil Dev established a new record for the highest number of Test wickets in a calendar year in 1979, whose record did he beat?

29. Which bowler, in 1976, took his 100th Test wicket in the record time of two years, 144 days?

30. Who was the first West Indian bowler to perform the hat trick in Test cricket?

31. When Richard Collinge dismissed Ian Botham in the third Test in 1977-78 and took his 112th wicket, a New Zealand record in Test cricket, whose record did he beat?

32. Who are the only father and son to have scored centuries on their Test debuts?

33. Who is the only batsman to score four Test centuries before his twenty-first birthday?

34. Who was the first batsman to score a century in Prudential Trophy matches?

i   In this Test match at Lord's in 1930, what (then) records was this batsman establishing at the time?

TENTH QUIZ: RECORDS

35. One of the two Australians who scored a century and a double century in the same Test match was Greg Chappell: who was the other?

36. Who is the only batsman to have scored fifty sixes in a season — and has, amazingly, done so on four occasions?

37. (a) Who shared the longest last-wicket partnership in first-class cricket?
    (b) How many runs did they make and against whom?

38. What is the highest number of runs scored by a batsman in one day in a Test match? Who scored them, where and when?

39. What is the highest first-wicket partnership in Australia?

40. Who scored 211 for Cambridge v Oxford in 1957?

41. Which batsman holds the record for the highest individual innings for Yorkshire?

42. Who scored most Test runs for South Africa?

43. Who, in the second Test with England in 1980, scored the highest individual innings by a West Indian at Lords?

44. Who are the only three men to have scored more than 3,500 runs in a first-class season?

45. Who were the first two players to have scored 1,000 Test runs in a calendar year more than once?

46. Who is the only Australian to have taken seventeen wickets in a first-class match in Australia?

47. Which man scored the fastest ever century in the Gillette Cup?

TENTH QUIZ: RECORDS

48. Which batsman holds the distinction of being the only man to have shared in two partnerships of over 500 in first-class cricket? Both, incidentally, were unbroken.

49. Which umpire retired in 1955, having stood in a record forty-eight Test matches?

50. Who played only one first-class innings in his career even though it yielded a double century?

51. Who was the first wicketkeeper to score 500 runs in a Test rubber?

52. Which pair of opening batsmen hold the record for the most century opening stands — sixty-nine in all?

53. Which batsman has scored the highest individual innings for an Australian touring team in a first-class match in Britain? When and against whom?

54. Who in the Lords Test of 1956, became the first wicketkeeper to dismiss nine batsmen in one Test?

55. (a) Which player has performed the highest number of first-class hat tricks?
    (b) How many?

56. Which batsman holds the record for having scored the highest number of runs in a calendar month?

57. Who held a catch whilst on the field for only one ball of a first-class match?

58. Who, in the second Test in 1962, became the first Pakistani to score a Test century in England?

59. Who was the first man to take 100 Test catches?

60. Which county holds the record for having had no fewer than seven brothers from the same family playing for it?

ii One of the least welcome sights for a nervous batsman — who is this bowler?

ELEVENTH QUIZ
THE LAWS

1. When may a batsman retire?

2. May drinks be taken during the last hour of a match?

3. Does the ball become 'dead' when a wicket is broken?

4. What is the overall width of a wicket?

5. What is the distance between the bowling and popping creases?

6. When does the ball cease to be 'dead'?

7. Does the ball become 'dead' upon lodging in the striker's pad?

8. In a two-day match what is the lead required to enforce the follow-on?

9. What is the penalty for fielding a ball with a cap?

10. What is the maximum length of a cricket bat?

11. When is a batsman's innings deemed to commence?

12. May a side bat with twelve men?

13. May a batsman be 'Out — caught' off a ball legitimately hit twice?

14. Is an appeal valid if made after 'Over' has been called?

15. May a valid catch be made if the ball rebounds from a tree sited inside the boundary line?

16. If covers are brought into use after play has commenced, what is the maximum distance they may extend in front of the popping crease?

17. What is the width of a turf pitch?

18. How long is the popping crease?

19. When do the umpires change ends?

20. What is the maximum height of a properly pitched wicket?

21. What happens if a fieldsman calls 'Lost ball'?

22. If the striker is 'Out — hit wicket' does the bowler get credit for the wicket?

23. When may a batsman who has retired injured resume his innings?

24. Has the batting captain the right to object to a substitute who is a specialist slip fielder being used to field in the slips

25. May a pitch be changed during the course of a match?

26. If the ninth wicket of the innings in progress falls at 4.05p.m. and tea is scheduled for 4.30p.m., when will tea be taken?

27. List the ways in which either batsman may be 'out' off a 'wide ball'.

28. In windy conditions may the captains agree to dispense with the use of bails?

29. May the captain who wins the toss elect to have the pitch rolled before the start of the match?

ELEVENTH QUIZ: THE LAWS

30. May the non-striker stand on the same side of the wicket as that from which the bowler is delivering?

31. What are the legal dimensions of a Grade One cricket ball?

32. What are the ten ways in which a batsman may be dismissed?

33. What is the Law concerning the limitation of fieldsmen on the on side of the wicket?

34. Once the captains have exchanged lists of nominated players and the toss has taken place, may the composition of a team be changed?

35. If weather conditions are unacceptable to the umpires, do the captains have the right to agree to play?

36. What should happen when both umpires call and signal 'One short' when the batsmen have completed three runs?

37. What are the seven occasions when the ball becomes 'dead' automatically?

38. What are the four basic questions which an umpire must be able to answer in the affirmative before he is justified in giving the striker 'Out — LBW' from a delivery which he has made a genuine attempt to play?

39. What conditions must be met by a captain wishing to forfeit his side's second innings?

40. What are the requirements regarding the placement of a bowler's feet for a delivery to be 'fair'?

41. What are three instances when an umpire would be

justified in calling 'Dead ball' whilst the batsmen were in the act of running?

42. What must the umpire do when a ball, which he considers to have been properly delivered, comes to rest three-quarters of the way down the pitch in front of the striker and, while the striker is advancing with the intention of striking the ball, a fieldsman dashes in and picks it up?

43. When a sharp shower occurs, if the wicketkeeper removes the bails from his wicket and the fielding side dash for cover whereas the batsmen stand their ground, what should the umpires do?

44. Define a wicket.

45. In what circumstances, other than foot faulting by the bowler, is the umpire at the bowler's end required to call 'No ball'?

46. What should the umpire do if both the batsmen commence to run while the bowler commences his run-up prior to delivery?

47. Is the captain of the side batting last in a match within his rights to complain if the fielding side are about to use an old ball at the start of his side's innings?

48. What should the umpire do if he suspects that the bowler at his end is lifting the seam of the ball?

49. If as the bowler shapes to attempt a return catch the non-striker calls out 'I bet he drops it!', what should the umpire do when the bowler duly misses the catch and then makes an appeal?

50. In accordance with the Law, a batsman may be given

'Out — handled the ball' if he wilfully touches the ball whilst it is in play. What are three occasions on which the umpire would be justified in declining such an appeal, even though the batsman had deliberately touched a ball in play with his hand?

TWELFTH QUIZ
EXTRAS

1. What do the Australians call what the English call 'extras'?

2. Harold Larwood had to retire 'hurt' during the Notts-Northants game in 1932: how did he hurt himself?

3. Why must September 1923 seem to have come particularly late to A.E.R. Gilligan?

4. B.B. Nimbalkar of Maharashtra was on his way to a world record score in 1948-49. He was on 443 not out against Kathiawar. Why did he not progress any further?

5. Why would the Kent all-rounder of the 1840's, Nicholas Felix, have been truly grateful for a pocket calculator?

6. Who caused play to be held up for a while during the 1974 Notts v Indian tourists match?

7. The 1868 game between Surrey and Lancashire was stopped for an hour. For what unlikely reason — unlikely in England that is — was it stopped?

8. Jim Laker's first wicket in first-class cricket came about in strange circumstances. He was bowling to R.N. Exton of the Combined Services who hit it down to short leg where it was caught by Alf Gover. What was odd about the dismissal?

9. What was odd about Mike Hendrick's dismissal of S. Madan Lal in the Old Trafford Test in 1974?

i What was the occasion of this short occupation of the crease?

TWELFTH QUIZ: EXTRAS

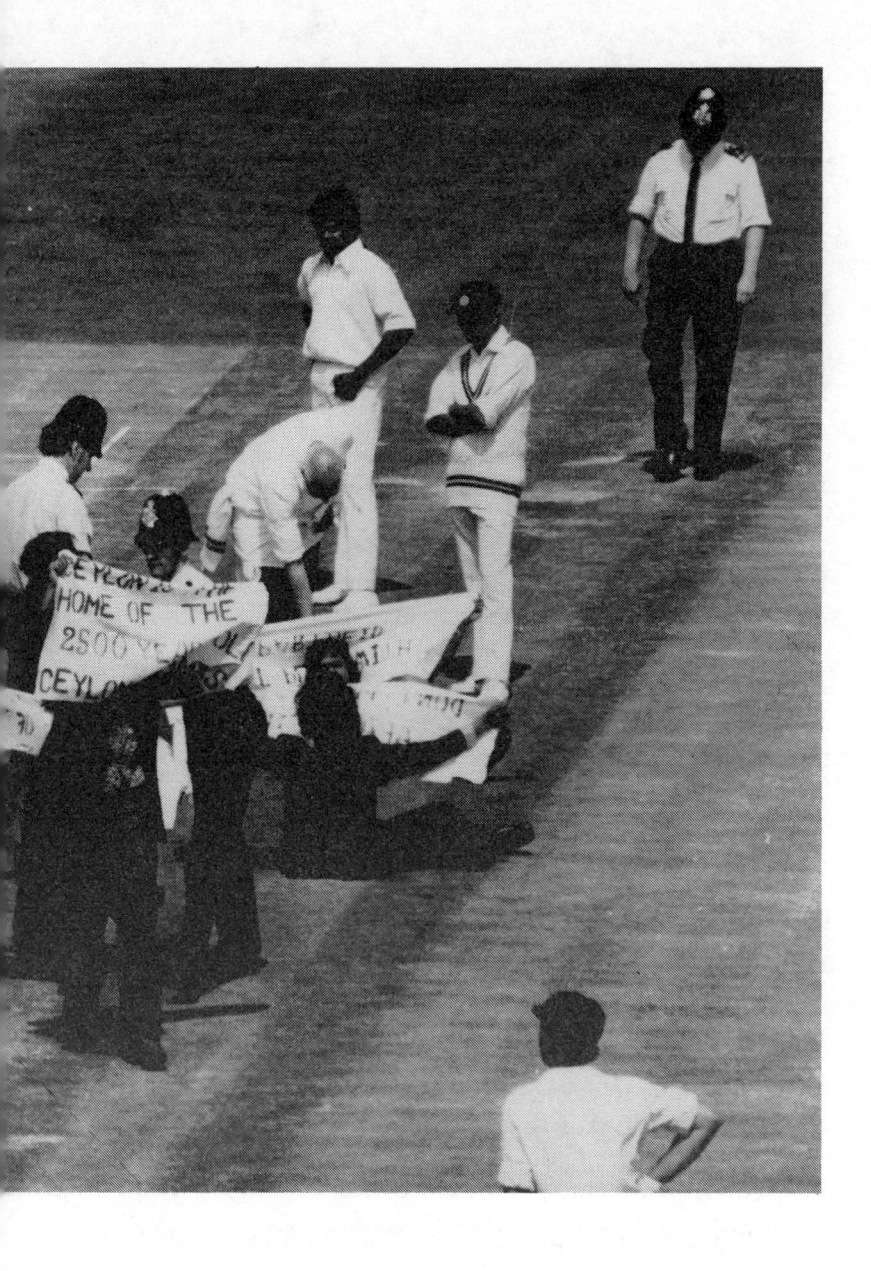

10. H.G. Vivian and his son G.E. Vivian both played for New Zealand. What, apart from their relationship, was unusual about their selection?

11. How was a promising start not fulfilled by a team led by G.O. Allen?

12. Why did Jimmy Binks have an enforced holiday in 1961-62?

13. Why might Geoff Cope have had just a twinge of regret over Mike Brearley's sportsmanship in 1977-78?

14. Who was the first substitute in first-class cricket to take a wicket as a bowler?

15. Why did the 1979 match between Lancashire and Derbyshire have to be restarted after three overs?

16. Whose son protested at the burden of bearing his father's cricketing fame by changing his surname?

17. Why was the start of the Worcestershire-Somerset match in 1979 delayed for one and a half hours?

18. Why were five runs added to Lancashire's total in the 1980 'Roses' match at Old Trafford?

19. Who missed his first Championship match for nineteen years, but on the second day's play was called on to the pitch as substitute and ended up captaining the side?

20. (a) What, in cricketing terms, is the 'Nelson'?
    (b) Why do Australians dislike the score 87?

21. For which country did K.S. Duleepsinjhi play Test cricket?

22. Why would Edward Lear or William McGonagle have

TWELFTH QUIZ: EXTRAS

appreciated the dismissal of Dennis Lillee in the second innings of the first Test with England in 1979-80?

23. Which team, in 1978-79, suffered its first defeat in thirty-two matches when beaten by MCC?

24. In which cities are the following Test grounds?
    (a) Bourda
    (b) Eden Gardens
    (c) The Exhibition Ground
    (d) The Gaddafi Stadium
    (e) Sabina Park
    (f) The Brabourne Stadium
    (g) The Wankhede Stadium
    (h) The Gabba
    (i) Eden Park

25. When the last fielder to take eight catches in a County Championship match did so in 1970, which Glamorgan player was it who caught the eight Derbyshire batsmen?

26. (a) In 1980-81 which Indian equalled Ian Chappell's achievement of seventy-one consecutive Test match appearances?
    (b) How many consecutive Tests did he eventually play?

27. Which player did Australia include in their party to tour Pakistan in 1980 — four years after his last Test appearance

28. Colin Cowdrey was one of the two men sent out to Australia and New Zealand on the 1974-75 tour as replacements for the injured batsmen — who was the second?

29. Of the two South Australian players in the Australian side which toured Britain in 1948, Bradman was one but who was the other?

ii   What is this trophy?

TWELFTH QUIZ: EXTRAS

30. Why did F.R. Spofforth refuse to play against England in the first Test at Melbourne in 1877?

31. Three years prior to joining Hampshire in 1968, for which county did Barry Richards play one game, which was, ironically, against the South Africans?

32. Who was the only survivor from the 1960-61 India-Pakistan Test series who played in the 1978 series — the first between the two countries since 1960-61?

33. Who missed the 1977 Benson & Hedges Cup final because he was 'cup tied', having played for another team in an earlier round?

iii One of the most famous, or infamous, personalities ever to 'appear' at Lord's — but what was his name, and when did he streak over the stumps?

34. For which Yorkshireman was a memorial fund established in 1946, which raised £8,233?

35. When England won twenty-six matches without defeat between 1968 and 1971, who was the only man to play in all twenty-six matches?

36. Who was the Indian player touring England in 1946 who became the first after the Second World War to perform the double of 1,000 runs and 100 wickets while on tour?

37. Who was the English batsman run out by Ewan Chatfield in the second England-New Zealand Test in 1977-78 when he was backing up?

38. Why is this known in Australia as being 'Mankaded'?

39. What is the name of the man whose supporters dug up the pitch at Headingley during the 1977 Test?

40. Who beat Marsden, the great Sheffield batsman, in single wicket matches at Norwich and Sheffield in the 1830s?

FIRST QUIZ
ANSWERS

1. Melbourne Cricket Ground
2. The Imperial Cricket Museum at Lord's
3. Corfu
4. Gentlemen v Players
5. It was donated by Lord Sheffield after the tour of Australia he had organized in 1891-92
6. Four
7. No
8. They are all wandering clubs, with no home grounds
9. Holland
10. D.W. Gregory
11. Gibraltar
12. South Africa
13. Australia and the West Indies
14. New South Wales and South Australia
15. Paris
16. United States and Canada
17. Bombay and Johannesburg
18. Napier (New Zealand)
19. England (second Test against Australia at Brisbane, 1982-83)
20. Derbyshire, Gloucestershire, Kent, Lancashire, Middlesex, Notts, Surrey, Sussex, Yorkshire
21. The 'Bat and Ball'
22. Kenya and Zimbabwe
23. (a) W.G. Grace (e) George Headley
    (b) E.M. Grace (f) H.D.G. Leveson-Gower
    (c) F.R. Spofforth (g) C.T.B. Turner
    (d) W.W. Armstrong (h) R.W. Marsh
24. Stamford Bridge (Chelsea FC)
25. Arundel
26. England and New Zealand
27. Bristol
28. Carmarthenshire, Denbighshire and Monmouthshire
29. 1886 to the USA and Canada
30. Albert Trott (July 1899)
31. (a) 1936 Indian team: the Maharajah of Vizianagram
    (b) Lala Amarnath
32. Sri Lanka

33. *John Jackson: Notts and All England*
34. *Jim Higgs with thirty-eight wickets at 18.65 in 1979-80*
35. *The White Heather Club*
36. *Broadhalfpenny and Windmill Downs*
37. *Highbury Stadium (Arsenal FC)*
38. *Kent and Surrey, 1709, Dartford Brent*
39. *Taunton*
40. *The Star and Garter Club*
41. *Marylebone Cricket Club (MCC)*
42. *John Small (Hambledon-Surrey, 1775)*
43. *Parliament had sanctioned the building of the Regents Canal through the old ground*
44. *(a) 1918-19   (b) 1979-80*
45. *Worcester*
46. *Peter — the Lord's cat (when he died at the age of fourteen in 1965)*
47. *Norman O'Neill*
48. *Phoenix Park*
49. *The first known Code of Laws was drawn up by the London Club. The first great match for which a full scorecard survives was played (Kent-All England at the Artillery Ground, Finsbury)*
50. *A.C. Bannerman and W.L. Murdoch*

i   *Back row: J. Conway (manager), G.H. Bailey, E. Gibbs, F.C. Allen*
Middle row: H.F. Boyle, W.L. Murdoch, T. Horan, D.W. Gregory, A.C. Bannerman, F.R. Spofforth
Front row: T.W. Garrett, C. Bannerman, J.McC. Blackham

ii   *(a) The 'Bodyline' tour of 1932-33*
(b) Sir Pelham Warner (left) and Douglas Jardine

iii *The Lord's Test v West Indies in 1963. When the ninth wicket fell in their second innings, England needed four to win with two balls left, and the only man left was Cowdrey, who had earlier retired hurt with a broken arm. In the event his partner, David Allen, played both balls away for a draw*

iv *(a) Learie Constantine*
(b) Dr C.B. Clarke

v   *S.C. Griffith (left) and Maurice Allom, respectively Secretary and Chairman of the Cricket Council in 1970 after discussing with Mr Jim Callaghan, the Home Secretary, the proposed tour to England by South Africa. It was later called off because of fears of disruption by anti-apartheid demonstrators*

SECOND QUIZ

1. Gary Sobers
2. Mushtaq Mohammed
3. Bob Willis
4. Frank Woolley, W.G. Grace, Tony Lock, Wally Hammond and Brian Close
5. The Nawab of Pataudi (Junior)
6. Bob Taylor
7. John Hampshire
8. Brian Close
9. Len Pascoe
10. Roy Tattersall
11. Bill Athey
12. Tony Pigott
13. Alan Jones (Glamorgan)
14. Dennis Lillee
15. Herbert Sutcliffe
16. Dave Gregory
17. Gilbert Jessop
18. Bobby Simpson
19. Staffordshire
20. Ian Johnson
21. Ken Higgs and John Snow
22. Brian Close and John Edrich
23. 'Titch' Freeman (1920's)
24. Kapil Dev
25. Dennis Lillee
26. David Steele
27. Denis Compton, because he appeared in advertisements for Brylcreem hair cream
28. (a) Lord Hawke (1883-1910)
    (b) He was not born in the county but in Lincolnshire

29. Graham McKenzie
30. (a) Robin Jackman (b) Alan Ward
31. Ian Botham
32. Bill Woodfull
33. Roy Swetman
34. They are/were all left-handed batsmen and right-handed bowlers
35. Mary Pilling
36. Bob Woolmer
37. Brian Close
38. Littleborough
39. Alec Bedser
40. (a) Robin Jackman (b) Alan Gibson
41. India (Kanpur)
42. Sam Trimble
43. Neil Harvey
44. Hanif, Mushtaq, Wasir, Zadiq
45. 'Fot'
46. Mike Brearley
47. (a) Greg Chappell (b) After the fifth Test in 1977
48. Freddie Brown
49. W.G. Grace
50. Peter May (20)
51. Nick Pocock (Hants)
52. Viv Richards — he disagreed with being given out, and as he threw his bat down it bounced off something and through the window
53. Hearne (A and GG for England, F for South Africa)
54. Joe Hardstaff (1946 v India)
55. Denis Compton
56. Ted Dexter
57. Tom Graveney (24,744 in the 1950's)
58. Patsy Hendren (28,711 in the 1920's)
59. Tony Lock (1,857 in the 1950's)
60. Brian McKechnie
61. (a) Arthur Fagg
    (b) Because of dissent shown by West Indian captain Rohan Kanhai when Fagg did not uphold an appeal, in the second Test between England and West Indies
62. Jim Burke
63. Keith Andrew

ANSWERS

64. *Geoff Pullar (1959 v India)*
65. *(a) Clive Lloyd   (b) 1980*
66. *Godfrey Evans (60)*
67. *(a) V.S. Hazare   (b) 1947-48, v Australia*
68. *Clyde Walcott*
69. *Trevor Bailey*
70. *Max Walker*
71. *Lance Gibbs*
72. *Herbert Sutcliffe*
73. *John Snow*
74. *Ray Illingworth and Ted Dexter*
75. *Imtiaz Ahmed*
76. *Tony Lewis (1972-73)*
77. *Mike Procter*
78. *'Dusty' Rhodes*
79. *(a) J.H. Parks and J.M. Parks*
    (b) Jim Parks senior scored over 3,000 runs and took more than 100 wickets
    (c) 1937
80. *John Wisden, North v South, Lord's 1850*
81. *M.G. Burgess, B.E. Congdon and V. Pollard, Lord's 1973; J.J. Crowe, I.D.S. Smith and J.G. Wright, Auckland, 1983-84*
82. *Sir Frank Worrell*
83. *(a) The Hon. Tim Lamb*
    (b) Oxford, Middlesex and Northamptonshire
84. *Derek Shackleton*
85. *Bruce Murray and Vic Pollard*
86. *George Sharp*
87. *(a) For the fastest first-class hundred in the English season*
    (b) Les Ames (1936 & 1939)
88. *(a) Imran Khan   (b) Richard Hadlee*
    (c) Shuja-ud-Din   (d) Mushtaq Mohammed
89. *Terry Jenner*
90. *Trevor Bailey*
91. *Greg Chappell*
92. *Norman 'Tufty' Mann*
93. *Haslingden*
94. *Bob Barber*
95. *M.P. (Monty) Bowden (aged 23 years 144 days in 1888-89)*
96. *W.G. Grace's mother*
97. *Tom Graveney, who was 41 when he made 118 at Port of*

Spain in January 1968
98. *J.W.H.T. Douglas (1924)*
99. *Timur Mohammed*
100. *Ray Illingworth*
101. *Graham Yallop, 1982-83 with 1,254*
102. *Jack Crapp (1948-49)*
103. *Richie and John Benaud*
104. *Both led the county to five County Championship successes, Surridge between 1952 and 1956, Shuter in 1887, 1888, 1890, 1891 and 1892 (they were also joint champions under his leadership in 1889)*
105. *Dermot Monteith*
106. *Rick McCosker*
107. *A.H.H. (Harold) Gilligan*
108. *They were Hutton's three Test victims as a bowler*
109. *Charles Macartney*
110. *Joel Garner*
111. *R. Nanan*
112. *Mick Malone*
113. *Leslie Hylton*
114. *George Gunn and Wilfred Rhodes*
115. *Jack Simmons (Lancashire, 1980)*
116. *Bobby Simpson*
117. *Donald Oslear*
118. *Ray Lindwall*
119. *Geoff Hurst, who scored a hat trick for England at football in the 1966 World Cup final, played one first-class game for Essex against Lancashire 1962. He scored 0 and 0 not out.*
120. *Gavin Byron Stevens*
121. *Peter Heine*
122. *Ossie Wheatley*
123. *'Horseshoe' (H.L. Collins)*
124. *W.G. Grace*
125. *Jim Burke of Australia*

i   *Denis Compton*
ii *Graeme Pollock, with Ron Hooker*
iii *Wally Grout*
iv *Bill Voce*
v   *Gary Sobers has Basil D'Oliviera caught by Faroukh Engineer, watched by Eddie Barlow in the First 'Test' between England*

and the Rest of the World. The series replaced the scheduled tour by South Africa cancelled as a result of the refusal of the South African government to let an England team containing the coloured D'Oliviera tour in 1968-69

vi Brian Yuile batting, with Vic Pollard. The bowler is Fred Titmus, the wicketkeeper Jim Parks, and Colin Cowdrey is at slip
vii Wes Hall
viii (a) B.S. Chandresekhar   (b) C.S. Elliott
ix Left to right: Tom Veivers (hidden), Alan Connolly, Doug Walters, Neil Hawke, Bob Cowper, Paul Sheahan, Barry Jarman, Graham McKenzie, Bill Lawry (captain)

THIRD QUIZ

Players 1
1. (b)
2. (f)
3. (d)
4. (g)
5. (c)
6. (i)
7. (h)
8. (e)
odd one out: (a) Clive Lloyd

Players 2
1. (i)
2. (d)
3. (e)
4. (h)
5. (g)
6. (a)
7. (b)
8. (c)
odd one out: (f) Tony Lock

Countries
1. (a)
2. (h)
3. (f)
4. (g)
5. (d)
6. (c)
7. (b)
8. (e)
odd one out: (i) Kenya

Grounds
1. (b)
2. (a)
3. (f)
4. (d)
5. (i)
6. (c)
7. (h)
8. (g)
odd one out: (e)Durban

FOURTH QUIZ

1. India
2. Graeme Wood
3. Victoria by MCC
4. Keith Miller
5. Graham Gooch
6. Northants
7. South Africa (thirty against England at Port Elizabeth, 1895-96; thirty against England at Edgbaston, 1924; thirty-five against England at Cape Town, 1898-99; thirty-six against Australia at Melbourne, 1931-32)
8. Hampshire (against Warwickshire at Edgbaston in 1922)
9. Jim Higgs (of Australia) in 1975
10. The Minor Counties
11. Eddie Paynter
12. Les Favell
13. (a) Border (b) 1959-60
14. (a) Alan Jones (Glamorgan) (b) None
15. India (against the West Indies)
16. Northants
17. (a) L. O'B. Fleetwood-Smith
    (b) The Oval Test 1938
18. Dilip Vengsarkar
19. Frank Hayes (Lancashire)
20. Ken Eastwood
21. Ralph Gosein
22. Thirty-five against New South Wales
23. Lance Cairns
24. Graham McKenzie
25. (a) England, Sydney 1920-21 to Headingley, 1921 (eight defeats) and South Africa, also eight defeats, Port Elizabeth 1888-89 to Cape Town 1898-99, their first eight Tests
    (b) New Zealand: Christchurch 1929 to Wellington 1955-56, their first forty-four Test matches

26. *Gladstone Small (Warwickshire-Middlesex)*
27. *M.L. Jaisimha, 1960-61, India-Pakistan, took his score from five not out to fifty-four not out*
28. *K.D. McKay*
29. *Twelve (Oxford-MCC and Ground, Oxford 1877). Twelve (Northants-Gloucestershire at Gloucester, 1907). Some would also like to add the six totalled by the B's, with one man absent, against England at Lord's in 1810*
30. *He prevented the wicketkeeper from catching him*
31. *Arthur Chipperfield*
32. *He was dismissed for a pair in successive balls. He was last man out, Glamorgan followed on and he was dismissed first ball*
33. *Dennis Breakwell (the balls were not in the same over)*
34. *Worcestershire (two Benson & Hedges and two Gillette Cup)*
35. *S.F.A. Bacchus (West Indies-India, 1978-79)*
36. *Rodney Hogg (in 1978-79 against Australia)*
37. *A.A. Mailey against England at Adelaide in 1920-21 with ten for 302 and against England at Sydney in 1924-25 with seven for 308*
38. *Bob Willis*
39. *Geoff Boycott (against Australia, first Test in 1979-80)*
40. *Peter Sainsbury (1971)*
41. *Eric Hollies*
42. *Ken Higgs (Leicestershire-Surrey)*
43. *Colin Cowdrey*
44. *R.E. Redmond (New Zealand)*
45. *Staffordshire*
46. *Colin Croft*
47. *Northants (1969 to 1974)*
48. *Somerset (1976)*
49. *Jim Foat (Gloucestershire)*
50. *Because of the outbreak of the French Revolution a team from Surrey had to cancel a tour to Paris*

i   *David Constant (left) and Harold Bird on the Saturday of the Centenary Test at Lord's in 1980 when they ruled the ground unfit after heavy rain the night before but on a hot, sunny day. Constant became involved in a scuffle with an MCC member on the steps of the pavilion*

FIFTH QUIZ

1. Imran Khan
2. Denis Compton
3. (a) Leeds
   (b) Don Bradman two, J.H. Edrich one
4. R.B. Simpson (311 at Old Trafford, 1964)
5. Bill Alley
6. Herbert Sutcliffe
7. Arthur Wellard
8. Kim Hughes
9. Glenn Turner, 43 not out, out of 131 v England at Lord's, 1969 and 223* out of 386 v West Indies at Kingston, 1971-72
10. Zadiq and Mushtaq Mohammed (v New Zealand, 1976)
11. Denis Compton, 1947
12. Harold Larwood
13. Glenn Turner
14. Ken Barrington
15. Barry Richards
16. Andrew Hilditch
17. David Lloyd (Lancashire)
18. (a) Graham Roope
    (b) 1977
19. Don Bradman (1930, 1934 and 1938)
20. Sydney cricket ground against the Indian touring team 1947-48
21. Robin Hobbs
22. Rhodesia
23. Mark Proctor
24. Ken Barrington (achieved the feat in 1964-65)
25. (a) Ian Botham
    (b) Because of a total eclipse of the sun
26. David Sheppard
27. (a) Bob Taylor
    (b) Geoff Miller
28. (a) Denis Compton, Adelaide, 1946/47
    (b) Arthur Morris

ANSWERS

29. *Clem Hill*
30. *Conrad Hunte*
31. *Lala Amarnath*
32. *Dennis Amiss, 203 v West Indies, The Oval, 1976*
33. *Maurice Leyland*
34. *Myrtle Maclagan (England, 119)*
35. *Jim Burke*
36. *Everton Weekes*
37. *Denis Compton, Bill Edrich, Len Hutton, Joe Hardstaff (Junior)*
38. *Patsy Hendren*
39. *Zaheer Abbas*
40. *Victor Trumper, C.G. Macartney, Don Bradman, Majid Khan*
41. *Don Bradman (334 at Headingley, 1930)*
42. (a) *Viv Richards*
    (b) *Glenn Turner*
43. *Joe Hardstaff (Junior) and Maurice Leyland*
44. *John Murray*
45. *Enid Bakewell*
46. *Dennis Lillee, 335*
47. *Lance Gibbs, 309*
48. *Brian Statham*
49. (a) *F.R. Spofforth took fourteen wickets for ninety in the match*
    (b) *It gave rise to the Ashes, following a mock obituary of English cricket in the* Sporting Times
50. *Lance Gibbs*
51. *R.G. Nadkarni v England 1963-64 at Madras*
52. *Eddie Barlow*
53. *Sarfraz Nawaz*
54. *Ray Illingworth*
55. *Hedley Verity (Yorkshire)*
56. *Imran Khan, with eighty-eight between 22 March 1982 and 4 February 1983*
57. *George Lohmann (England)*
58. *Joel Garner*
59. *Ireland*
60. *Derek Shackleton*
61. *Alec Bedser*

62. Richard Collinge
63. Dilip Doshi
64. Richard Collinge
65. Bob Willis (moved to Warwickshire in 1972)
66. Tony Lock
67. J. Bart King of Philadelphia
68. Ian Johnson
69. Wally Hammond
70. Johnny Briggs (England v South Africa 1888-89)
71. W.W. Davis (West Indies v Australia, 1983, Leeds, 7 for 51)
72. Peter Loader (1957 v West Indies)
73. Ken Smales (10 for 66, Notts v Gloucestershire at Stroud)
74. Dick Motz (New Zealand)
75. N.B.F. Mann (South Africa v England, Trent Bridge, 1947)
76. Rodney Marsh
77. John Lever
78. Fred Swarbrook (Derbyshire v Sussex, 1975)
79. Eddie Gilbert, for Queensland at Brisbane, 1931-32)
80. S.J. Rixon
81. Jackie Hendriks
82. Taylor (Brian and Bob)
83. W.L. Cornford
84. Godfrey Evans
85. Gil Langley
86. Roger Tolchard
87. Jimmy Binks (Yorkshire)
88. Rodney Marsh, fifty-three
89. Don Tallon
90. Geoff Humpage
91. E.J.K. Burn
92. A.E. Dick
93. Arnold Long (Surrey v Sussex)
94. F.E. Woolley (deputizing for Les Ames in the second innings)
95. Sunil Gavaskar
96. Derek Underwood
97. Allan Border
98. W.G. Grace
99. Geoff Dymock
100. Charlie Hallows (1928)
101. Graeme Wood
102. W.G. Grace

103. Charlie Grimmett
104. Geoff Boycott (1st Test v Australia, 1979-80)
105. Mike Whitney
106. He took a wicket, that of Wasim Bari
107. Larry Gomes
108. (a) Lawrence Rowe
    (b) in 1973-74 v England at Bridgetown
109. Graham McKenzie
110. D.D. Blackie, aged 46 years 253 days, in 1928
111. Wayne Larkins
112. Intikhab Alam
113. C. Bannerman with 165* for Australia in the first ever Test in 1877
114. Bob Massie, at Lord's in 1972
115. G.R. Viswanath
116. (a) Greg Chappell
    (b) in 1973-74, v New Zealand
117. R.E. Foster, with 287 and 19 for England at Sydney 1903
118. Wally Hammond (1951)
119. Bandula Warnapura
120. Duleep Mendis, v India at Madras in 1982-83
121. Dick Motz
122. Graham McKenzie
123. Gary Sobers
124. Greg Chappell
125. Viv Richards, Desmond Haynes and Graeme Wood
126. Warren Bardsley, 136 and 130, v England at The Oval, 1909
127. Alec Bedser and Jack Ikin
128. Mike Selvey
129. G.E. Corling
130. Maurice Tate
131. Lee Irvine
132. Len Hutton
133. H. Ironmonger
134. R. Howorth (1947)
135. S.C. Griffith (v West Indies, 1947-48)
136. Chris Broad (Gloucestershire v Oxford University)
137. Canada
138. Viv Richards
139. Steve Smith
140. Fred Trueman

141. Denmark
142. Alan Hurst
143. Graeme Hick (Zimbabwe)
144. Allan Lamb
145. Paul Jarvis (Yorkshire)
146. Alan Turner, for Australia v Sri Lanka, 1975
147. Gordon Greenidge
148. Glenn Turner
149. Trevor Chappell, 110 v India, 1983
150. Clive Lloyd (Lancashire 1972 and 1975)
151. Bob Woolmer
152. Hertfordshire
153. Bruce Edgar
154. Zaheer Abbas
155. Kent
156. Lincolnshire (beat Glamorgan, 1974)
157. Mike Gatting
158. Geoff Boycott
159. Canada
160. B.A. Langford (Somerset)
161. David Gower
162. David Hughes
163. Sussex (1967-70)
164. Chris Old (Yorkshire v Derbyshire)
165. Leicestershire (1974)
166. Younis Ahmed (for Worcestershire v Surrey)
167. Essex
168. Scarborough (in the Haig final)
169. Frank Worrell
170. Richie Benaud
171. Tony Lewis
172. Douglas Jardine (1932-33)
173. Bill Woodfull
174. Ray Illingworth
175. Greg Chappell
176. Ted Dexter
177. Peter May
178. Kevin Sharpe
179. Kim Hughes (1979)
180. The Nawab of Pataudi (Senior)
181. A.H. Kardar

ANSWERS

182. Ian Botham (Brian Rose) and G.O. Allen (R.W.V. Robins)
183. Peter May (285 v West Indies, 1957)
184. Sir Murray Bisset, the captain of a South African team to visit England in 1901 during the Boer War
185. Ian Chappell
186. Denis Compton
187. Vic Richardson
188. Colin Cowdrey
189. Francis Thomas Mann (1922-23) and Francis George Mann (1948-49 and 1949)
190. Asif Iqbal
191. Ajit Wadekar
192. Tom Graveney and Barry Jarman
193. (a) Brian Rose
     (b) Somerset were expelled from the competition
194. Peter van der Merwe
195. Bobby Simpson (311 v England at Old Trafford, 1964)
196. Gary Sobers
197. Jim Watts
198. Dermot Montieth
199. John Barclay
200. (a) Arthur Conningham
     (b) A.E. Stoddart (in the second Test 1894-95)

i   (a) S.E. Gregory
     (b) He played in 58 Tests
     (c) His father Ned, his uncle Dave (Australian captain in the first Tests), and his cousin Jack
ii   (a) B.J.T. Bosanquet
     (b) Bosie and Googly
     (c) His son Reginald was an ITN newscaster
iii   Because it was one of Jim Laker's 19 victims at Old Trafford in 1956. Lock took the other wicket — only one, despite bowling unchanged throughout the second innings
iv   The Indian crowd during the 1983 final when India beat the West Indies to win the Prudential Cup
v   Wally Hammond (England) and Lindsay Hassett (Australia)

SIXTH QUIZ

1. John Arlott
2. Bill Lawry
3. Conrad Hunte
4. C.B. Fry
5. Frank Tyson
6. Squash
7. Fred 'The Demon' Spofforth
8. Politics
9. Arthur Milton and Willie Watson
10. Sam Loxton
11. Ken Grieves
12. Paul Downton
13. Derek Pringle
14. Brian Booth
15. Trevor Bailey
16. Arthur Mailey
17. Sir Robert Menzies
18. Colin Croft
19. Robert Peel
20. Dave Gregory
21. M.J.K. Smith
22. Norman Yardley
23. G.C. Grant
24. Sir Frank Worrell
25. Ali Bacher
26. Noel Cantwell (Manchester United and Ireland)
27. Harold Makepeace (Everton and Lancashire)
28. Rupert 'Spook' Hanley
29. Roland Butcher
30. Arthur Milton
31. Ian Redpath
32. Nawab of Pataudi (Senior)
33. Sir C. Aubrey Smith
34. John Warr
35. Percy McDonnell: 'Greatheart'

36. *R.E. Foster*
37. *Paul Sheahan*
38. *Ted Dexter*
39. *Clive Van Ryneveld*
40. *Colin McDonald*
41. *Aftab Gul*
42. *Phil Mead*
43. *Wally Hammond*
44. *J.W.H.T. Douglas*
45. *Rackets (also a good Real Tennis player)*
46. *Dr R.H.B. ('Reg') Bettington*
47. *Peter May*
48. *Donald Ford*
49. *Hockey*
50. *Maurice Allom*

i *Gary Sobers, who made the world Test record 365* in ten hours in 1957-58*

SEVENTH QUIZ

1. *(a) Glamorgan   (b) 1921*
2. *Surrey*
3. *Yorkshire (1966/1967/1968)*
4. *Essex*
5. *Leicestershire*
6. *Brian Sellers*
7. *Fred Titmus (1971)*
8. *Tony Lock (1959)*
9. *Yorkshire*
10. *Geoff Boycott (1963)*
11. *Graham Gooch*
12. *Leicestershire & Yorkshire*
13. *Leicestershire (1975)*
14. *M.J.K. Smith (1959)*
15. *Glamorgan (587 for 8 in 1951)*

16. *Clive Lloyd*
17. *Wilfred Slack*
18. *Pat Pocock (Surrey v Sussex 1972)*
19. *Fred Titmus and Wilf Rhodes. (Note: several others have played first-class cricket in five decades but not in the County Championship)*
20. *Graham Stevenson*
21. *Peter Loader (Surrey v Warwickshire)*
22. *Jim Cumbes*
23. *Brian Statham*
24. *Fred Titmus (back to Middlesex from Surrey in 1979)*
25. *Middlesex (Lords was being used for the Eton-Harrow match at the time)*
26. *Ian Botham*
27. *Zaheer Abbas (1976)*
28. *Graham Johnson*
29. *Lancashire and Gloucestershire*
30. *Ken Higgs*
31. *Gloucestershire*
32. *Kent and Sussex, Hastings, 1984*
33. *Somerset*
34. *Worcestershire*
35. *A.W. Lilley (Essex v Notts)*
36. *Malcolm Nash*
37. *Last man to score 100 and perform the hat trick in a County Championship match*
38. *Yorkshire*
39. *Warwickshire; Norman McVicker*
40. *Northants (1967), Glamorgan (1979), Warwickshire (1982)*
41. *Graham Stevenson*
42. *Alvin Kallicharran*
43. *Gordon's Gin*
44. *Alen Connolly*
45. *Middlesborough*
46. *Edgbaston*
47. *Kent (Canterbury)*
48. *Bristol*
49. *St Helens, Swansea*
50. *Maidstone*
51. *Gloucestershire*
52. *(a) Victoria, 1,107 v New South Wales, 1926-27*

ANSWERS

(b) *South Australia, 27 v New South Wales, 1955-56*
53. Western Australia
54. David Hookes
55. Tony Grieg
56. New South Wales, Victoria and South Australia
57. New South Wales
58. Colin Milburn — they put on 328 v Queensland at Brisbane
59. Bill Woodfull
60. Les Favell, 8,983 (38.38)
61. Geoff Dymock (226)
62. Mervyn Waite
63. J.E.H. Hooker (New South Wales v Victoria 1928-29)
64. Clarrie Grimmett (1,424)
65. Sydney Cricket Ground
66. The winners of Sydney Grade cricket
67. John Inverarity
68. The Exhibition ground
69. The WACA, Perth
70. George Giffen
71. Brian Davison (Leics)
72. Bob Simpson
73. C.T.B. Turner, New South Wales, 1887-88
74. A.F. Kippax, 6,096 runs at 70.88
75. David Ogilvie, Queensland, 1977-78
76. Roger Woolley (1977-78)
77. Don Tallon (1938-39)
78. Kumar Shri Ranjitsinhji
79. Barbados
80. J.S. Hiddleston (Wellington 1923-24)
81. Barbados
82. Bombay
83. Griqualand West
84. Quaid-I-Azam Championship
85. Barbados, Guyana (British Guiana at the time), Jamaica, Trinidad and Combined Islands (Windward and Leeward Islands)
86. Glenn Turner
87. Western Province, Natal, Transvaal
88. E.H.C. Griffith — Jamaica (150 v Combined Islands)
89. Gary Sobers (204 v Guyana)
90. Bert Sutcliffe

91. *Graeme Pollock*
92. *New Zealand*
93. *South Africa*
94. *Auckland*
95. *Geoff Greenidge (not Gordon...), Barbados*
96. *A.D. Nourse Jnr (Natal)*
97. *Jack Cheetham and Eric Rowan*
98. *Denis Compton was in the Holkar side — he scored 249 not out*
99. *Jack Short*
100. *Italy*

i *The winning Kent 'twelve' at Lord's in 1967 (except Brian Luckhurst who is missing)*
Standing: Alan Knott, Mike Denness, John Shepherd, Derek Underwood, David Sayer (twelfth man), Norman Graham, Colin Cowdrey, Stuart Leary, Alan Dixon, Alan Brown
Sitting: Alan Ealham

EIGHTH QUIZ

1. *Peter Tinniswood*
2. *Ben Travers*
3. *Irving Rosenwater*
4. *Canada and the United States*
5. *Eric Beecher*
6. *Ray Robinson*
7. *E.W. Swanton*
8. *Charles Cundall*
9. *Mihir Bose*
10. *Mike Francis, Ivan Rose, Roger Towers and Ron Wootton*
11. *Jim Laker*
12. *George Giffen*
13. *Sir Neville Cardus*
14. Green Sprigs: Cricket's Age of Youth — *it was published first*

       under this title in 1954
15. E.H.D. Sewell, An Outdoor Wallah, *and Scyld Berry*, Cricket Wallah
16. *Tillingfold*
17. *Twenty-nine (in 1962)*
18. *Lionel Lord Tennyson*
19. *F.S. Ashley-Cooper*
20. *Bowls*
21. *Neville (later Sir Neville) Cardus in* Good Days
22. *Cricket Crisis, 1946*
23. *Sigfried Sassoon,* Dreamers
24. *Mike Brearley in* Phoenix from the Ashes
25. *Ruskin Spear*
26. *Harry Altham*
27. *'A Country Vicar'*
28. *James Thorpe himself*
29. *(a) 'Felix'   (b) The 'Catapulta', an early bowling machine*
30. *James Pycroft*
31. *E.V. Lucas*
32. *The 1958-59 series with England*
33. *A.J. Raffles*
34. *J.B. (later Sir Jack) Hobbs*
35. *A.A. Thomson's*
36. *A.W. Ledbrooke, author of* Lancashire County Cricket, 1864-1953
37. *David Frith, for* My Dear Victorious Stod
38. *H.M.S. Fury and H.M.S. Hecla*
39. *Arthur Mailey in* 10 for 66 and All That *of Victor Trumper*
40. *(a) A.W. Pullin, (b) J.A.H. Catton, (c) Harold Luke, and (d) R.T. Symond*
41. *Kenneth Farnes,* Tours and Tests
42. *W.H. Crockford, W.H. Knight, G.H. West, C.F. Pardon, S.H. Pardon, C. Stewart Caine, S.J. Southerton, W.H. Brookes, Haddon Whitaker, Hubert Preston, Norman Preston and John Woodcock. (Twelve in all)*
43. *(a) J.M. Barrie, (b) J.C. Squire, and (c) Tim Rice*
44. *C.P. Snow,* Time of Hope, *E.E. Snow, A History of Leicestershire Cricket and P.A. Snow,* Cricket on the Fiji Islands
45. *P.G.H. Fender,* The Turn of the Wheel: MCC Team, Australia 1928-9

46. *R.C. Robertson-Glasgow*
47. *Sir Arthur Conan Doyle*
48. *Alfred D. Taylor in 1903*
49. *Jack Pollard, of Kim Hughes, in* Australian Cricket: The Game and the Players
50. *Thomas Rowlandson*
51. *Ronald Mason*, Batsman's Paradise
52. *A.G. Moyes*, Australian Cricket: A History
53. A Song for Cricket *by David Rayvern Allen*
54. *R.S. Whitington*
55. *E.V. Lucas*, Good Days
56. *Norman Gale*, The Hope of Surrey
57. *Alfred Cochrane*, To Lucasta
58. *Lord Harris, in a letter to* The Times *on his eightieth birthday*
59. *Sir Home Gordon*, Cricket Form at a Glance, 1878-1937
60. *R.C. Robertson-Glasgow*, Wisden, *1944*

i *Archibald Stuart-Wortley, in 1891. The painting hangs at Lords*

NINTH QUIZ

1. *John Arlott*
2. *Arthur Wrigley*
3. *Australia*
4. *L.G. Watt (Australia v The Rest, Sydney 4 December 1925)*
5. *Brian Johnston (who else?)*
6. *Arthur Richardson was famous for frequently saying this to his ABC broadcasting colleague, Arthur Gilligan*
7. *Ian Chappell*
8. *Ian Chappell is Arthur Richardson's grandson*
9. *Because his name is Peter Sellers*
10. *Wendy Wimbush*
11. *Paul Parker*
12. *Rex Alston and Alan McGilvray*
13. *G.E. Gomez*
14. *Glenn Turner*

15. *John Arlott advertised them both*
16. *Michael Charlton*
17. *Charles Fortune (South Africa)*
18. *Neil Adcock*
19. *Alan Fairfax*
20. *Reverend F.H. Gillingham*
21. *H.B.T. Wakelam*
22. *I.A.R. Peebles*
23. *James D. Coldham*
24. *Martin Richard Cobbett, of the* Sportsman *1882-83*
25. *Richie Benaud*

i *Kerry Packer, sponsor of World Series cricket. Richie Benaud was one of his advisors*

TENTH QUIZ

1. *Hanif Mohammed*
2. *Garfield Sobers: 365* for West Indies v Pakistan, Kingston, 1957/58*
3. *Len Hutton's 364 for England v Australia at The Oval in 1938*
4. *Pakistan and India (run ended in 1978)*
5. *Bev Congdon (3,448)*
6. *John Edrich, 310 not out v New Zealand in 1965*
7. *Bob Cowper, 307 v England in 1965-66*
8. *Arthur Fagg: 244 and 202 not out for Kent v Essex at Colchester in 1938*
9. *Don Bradman at Lords, Leeds, Adelaide and Brisbane*
10. *Don Bradman*
11. *Wally Hammond v New Zealand at Auckland, 1932-33*
12. *Sunil Gavaskar (scored 1,984 between October 1978 and October 1979, beating Viv Richards' old record of 1,811)*
13. *Glenn Turner (Worcestershire v Glamorgan)*
14. *Kapil Dev (21 years, 27 days)*
15. *Glenn Turner (1973-74 v Australia)*
16. *Greg Chappell (631)*
17. *Pakistan (1st Test v West Indies 1976-77)*
18. *Lawrence Rowe (West Indies v New Zealand, 1971-72)*

19. *Wilfred Rhodes — 16*
20. *Gilbert Jessop (in 1902)*
21. *Jack Gregory, 70 minutes, v South Africa*
22. *W.H. Ponsford, Victoria, 429 v Tasmania in 1922-23 and 451 v Queensland in 1927-28*
23. *Vinoo Mankad's (23 games, to Botham's 21)*
24. *A.W. Wellard (Somerset, 1936 and 1938)*
25. *R.E. Foster (287 England v Australia, 1903)*
26. *Gul Mahomed and V.F. Hazare, 577, Baroda v Holkar, 1946-47*
27. *Sunil Gavaskar (India), v West Indies 1970-71, v Pakistan 1978-79 and v West Indies 1978-79*
28. *Graham McKenzie's*
29. *Andy Roberts*
30. *Wes Hall (v Pakistan 1958-59)*
31. *Bruce Taylor's*
32. *L. and S. Amarnath (India)*
33. *G.A. Headley (West Indies)*
34. *Dennis Amiss (103 v Australia, 1972)*
35. *Doug Walters (1968-69 v West Indies)*
36. *Arthur Wellard (Somerset: 1933-35-36-38)*
37. *(a) A.F. Kippax and J.E.H. Hooker*
    (b) 307 — New South Wales v Victoria, 1928-29
38. *309 — Don Bradman, for Australia against England, Headingley, 1930*
39. *456 — W.H. Ponsford and E.R. Mayne, Victoria v Queensland, 1923-24*
40. *Gami Goonesena*
41. *George Hirst, 341 v Leicestershire, 1905*
42. *Bruce Mitchell (3,471)*
43. *Desmond Haynes (184)*
44. *T.H. Hayward (1906), W.J. Edrich (1947), and D.C.S Compton (1947)*
45. *Ken Barrington in 1961 and 1963, and Sunil Gavaskar in 1976 and 1978 (he has in fact achieved the feat twice more since then)*
46. *George Giffen (South Australia v Victoria, 1885-86)*
47. *Roy Marshall (in 77 minutes for Hampshire v Bedfordshire, 1968)*
48. *Frank Worrell who put on 574* with Clyde Walcott, Barbados's 4th wicket in 1945/46 against Trinidad and 502**

with John Goddard, also for Barbados v Trinidad, in 1943/44
49. Frank Chester
50. N.F. Callaway (New South Wales 1914-15; he was to lose his life on active service during the war)
51. B.K. Kunderman (India v England, 1963-64)
52. Percy Holmes and Herbert Sutcliffe
53. C.G. Macartney, 345 v Nottinghamshire, 1921
54. Gil Langley (Australia)
55. (a) D.V.P. Wright (Kent)
    (b) Seven
56. Len Hutton (1,294 in 1949)
57. Mike Hall, Nottinghamshire v Middlesex, at Trent Bridge, 1955. He came out with incoming batsman Denis Compton to replace a fielder who had left to go to the toilet, caught Compton in the slips and returned to the pavilion.
58. Nasim-ul-Ghani
59. Wally Hammond
60. Worcestershire, or 'Fostershire' as it was known in the early years of the century on account of the Foster brothers

i   Don Bradman on his way to 254* — then the highest Test innings by anyone in England, and the highest for any Australian against England
ii Michael Holding

ELEVENTH QUIZ

1. At any time (Law 2.9)
2. No (Law 16.6)
3. No: unless a batsman is out thereby (Law 23.4)
4. Nine inches (Law 8)
5. Four feet (Law 9)
6. Upon the bowler commencing his run-up or bowling action (Law 23.3)
7. Yes (Law 23.1)
8. 100 runs (Law 13.1)

9. *Five runs are added to the run or runs already made. If no run has been scored five penalty runs are added (Law 41.1)*
10. *Thirty-eight inches (Law 6)*
11. *Once he has stepped on to the field of play (Law 2.10)*
12. *Yes. Provided there has been prior agreement between the captains before the toss (Law 1)*
13. *Yes. Provided the ball has not touched the ground since first being struck (Law 32.2(d))*
14. *Yes. Provided it is lodged prior to the bowler beginning his run-up or bowling action to deliver the first ball of the succeeding over (Law 27.1)*
15. *Yes. But only if the tree has not been previously agreed to be a boundary (Law 32.3(f))*
16. *Not further than four feet in front of the popping crease unless there has been prior agreement, or the regulations provide for total covering (Law 11)*
17. *Five feet either side of a line joining the centre of the middle stumps of the wickets: i.e. ten feet (Law 7.1)*
18. *Whilst it is marked to a minimum of six feet either side of the line of the wicket, the crease itself is deemed to be unlimited in length (Law 9)*
19. *After each side has had one innings (Law 3.11)*
20. *Twenty-eight and a half inches. Stumps twenty-eight inches and bails half an inch (Law 8)*
21. *Six runs are added to the score unless more than six runs have already been run before the call, in which case as many runs as have been completed shall be scored (Law 20)*
22. *Yes (Law 35)*
23. *At the fall of a wicket, or upon the retirement of another batsman (Law 2.9)*
24. *No (Law 2.2)*
25. *Only if it becomes unfit for play and then only with the agreement of both captains (Law 7.3)*
26. *As soon as the last wicket falls or at 5pm, whichever is the earlier (Law 16)*
27. *(Law 25) The striker may be out — Hit Wicket (Law 35) or Stumped (Law 39), and either batsman may be Run Out (Law 38), Handled the Ball (Law 33), or Obstructing the Field (Law 37)*
28. *No. It is for the umpires to decide (Law 8, note (a))*
29. *Only if the start of play is officially delayed after the toss for innings has been made (Law 10.1)*

ANSWERS

30. Only with the agreement of the bowler's end umpire (Law 22.8)
31. It shall weigh not less than five and a half ounces, and not more than five and three-quarter ounces. The circumference shall be not less than eight and thirteen-sixteenths of an inch and not more than nine inches (Law 5)
32. Bowled: Timed Out: Caught: Handled the Ball: Hit the Ball Twice: Hit Wicket: Leg Before Wicket: Obstructing the Field: Run Out, and Stumped (Laws 30-39 (inc))
33. No more than two on-side fieldsmen shall be behind the popping crease at the instant of the bowler's delivery (Law 41.2)
34. Only with the consent of the opposing captain (Law 1.2)
35. Yes. Provided they are both agreed (Law 3.8)
36. The umpires must confer to clarify which run each had called short. If both called the same run, only one run is disallowed, but if they called different runs then two runs are disallowed and the scorers advised accordingly (Law 18.2)
37. When the ball is finally settled in the hands of the wicketkeeper or the bowler
    When the ball reaches or pitches over the boundary.
    When a batsman is out
    Whether played or not, if the ball lodges in the clothing or equipment of a batsman or the clothing of an umpire
    When the ball lodges in the helmet of a fielder
    Upon the call of 'Over' or 'Time'
    Upon the award of a penalty for 'Lost Ball' or 'Illegal Fielding'
    (Law 23)
38. Did the ball pitch on a straight line between wicket and wicket, or on the off-side of the striker's wicket?
    Was it first intercepted by part of the striker's person, dress or equipment, other than his hand holding the bat?
    Was the point of impact in line between wicket and wicket even if above the level of the bails?
    Would the ball have hit the wicket if not intercepted? (Law 36)
39. His decision must be notified to the opposing captain and the umpires in sufficient time to allow seven minutes rolling of the pitch and the normal ten minutes interval between innings (Law 14)
40. In the delivery stride his back foot must land within and not touch either the return crease or its forward extension, and some part of his front foot must be behind the popping crease, whether grounded or raised (Law 24.3)
41. If either, or both, batsmen deliberately run short (Law 23.2)

In the event of serious injury to a player, or to his colleague (Law 18.2 (c))
Upon any attempt by the batsmen to steal a run during the bowler's run-up, unless the bowler throws the ball at either wicket (Law 42.12)

42. *Replace the ball where it came to rest*
Order the fieldsmen to resume the places they occupied prior to delivery of the ball
Allow the striker one attempt to strike the ball (Law 25.3)

43. *Confer together. If they agree that conditions are not suitable instruct the batsmen to retire to the pavilion, but inform the fielding captain that the umpires' consent to leave the field is always necessary. If they do not agree that conditions warrant the suspension of play, and they receive an appeal from the batting side, award the match to that side by default (Law 21.3)*

44. *A wicket shall be nine inches in width and consist of three wooden stumps of equal and sufficient size to prevent the ball from passing between them, with two bails on top. The tops of the stumps shall be twenty-eight inches above the ground and shall be dome-shaped except for the bail grooves. The bails are each four and three-eighths inches long and when in position shall project not more than half an inch above the stumps (Law 8)*

45. *If the bowler changes his mode of delivery without prior notification*
If the bowler's arm action is unfair
If a fieldsman encroaches onto or over the pitch before the striker has made contact with the ball, or it has passed his bat
If, prior to delivery, the bowler throws the ball at the striker's wicket in an attempt to run him out
If the bowler is guilty of persistent short pitching or the persistent bowling of fast high full pitches (Laws 24.1,2,4,5 and 41.3)

46. *Unless the bowler attempts to run out either batsman he will call and signal 'Dead ball' as soon as the batsmen have crossed and will then return them to their original ends. No runs are scored (Law 42.12)*

47. *Unless there has been agreement otherwise before the toss either captain may demand a new ball at the start of each innings (Law 5.3)*

48. *Consult with his colleague. If they agree that there has been*

interference with the seam, exchange the ball for one of similar condition to that in use prior to the contravention of the Law. Inform the batsmen of the change of ball and warn the fielding captain of the unfair practice (Law 5.3)

49. *The non-striker's call constitutes a verbal act of obstruction. Therefore, since the obstruction prevented a catch from being made,* the striker *must be given 'Out — Obstructing the Field' (Law 37.1,2)*

50. *If the hand was holding the bat at the moment of impact*
    If the striker receives a request from the fielding side to do so
    If he uses his hand to protect his person from being hit (Law 33)

TWELFTH QUIZ

1. *Sundries*
2. *When bowling, he caught his finger on the stumps and cut it so badly he could take no further part in the match!*
3. *He batted in a record seventy first-class innings that season*
4. *The opposing team refused to come out after lunch — they'd had enough!*
5. *He used to keep a note of his score by writing it on the front of his shirt!*
6. *Parachutists — they were supposed to be heading for the River Trent, but went off course and landed close to the pitch*
7. *Excessive heat!*
8. *Alf Gover caught the ball between his legs because he was putting his sweater on at the time*
9. *He knocked out the off and leg stumps, but the middle stump remained in place*
10. *H.G. Vivian was chosen to tour England after only three first-class matches, but his son went even better. His appearance in the second Test against India in 1965 was also his first-class debut*
11. *He led England to victory in the first two Tests in Australia in 1936-37, only to lose the next three*
12. *He was flown out to India and Pakistan to replace the injured John Murray, but did not play in a Test*

13. *He would have had a hat trick in his first Test, but Brearley recalled batsman Iqbal Qasim, saying the catch was 'not clean'*
14. *David Brown (Warwickshire-Lancashire, 1982)*
15. *It was discovered that the wickets were out of line*
16. *Bradman's son changed his name to Bradson*
17. *The starting handle fell off the roller and was embedded in the pitch. A new wicket had to be cut*
18. *The ball hit a protective helmet placed behind the Yorkshire wicketkeeper*
19. *Keith Fletcher (Essex)*
20. *(a) A score of 111*
    (b) It is thirteen less than 100
21. *England*
22. *Lillee was caught Willey, bowled Dilley*
23. *Western Australia*
24. *(a) Georgetown*
    (b) Calcutta
    (c) Brisbane
    (d) Lahore
    (e) Kingston
    (f) Bombay
    (g) Bombay
    (h) Brisbane
    (i) Auckland
25. *Peter Walker*
26. *(a) G.R. Viswanath*
    (b) Eighty-seven
27. *Ashley Mallett*
28. *Barry Wood*
29. *Ron Hamence*
30. *Because he wanted Murdoch rather than Blackham as wicketkeeper*
31. *Gloucestershire*
32. *Mushtaq Mohammed*
33. *Alistair Hignell — he had played for the Combined Universities*
34. *Hedley Verity*
35. *John Edrich*
36. *Vinoo Mankad*
37. *Derek Randall*
38. *Because in the second Test at Sydney in 1947-48 Vinoo Mankad ran out Bill Brown as he backed up, having done the same thing*

      to him earlier on the tour
39. *George Davies*
40. *Fuller Pilch*

i   *The Gillette Cup*
ii *Tamils protesting against alleged racism in Sri Lanka during the Australia v Sri Lanka Prudential Cup match at The Oval in 1975*
iii *Michael Angelow, 1975*

All photographs: Sport and General